A Beginner's Guide to...

Creative

Writing

For Sally, George, Ellie and Frankie

and

Steph Commons for teaching me so much.

Thanks Steph.

Creative writing is any writing that goes outside the bounds of normal professional, journalistic, academic, or technical forms of literature, typically identified by an emphasis on narrative craft, character development, and the use of literary tropes or with various traditions of poetry and poetics.

Just write…

Contents

PART ONE:
THE COMFORT ZONE
(and how to leave it)

When Stars Collide...

I am not fatalistic. I'm quite laissez-faire, lazy even. I have no sense of preordainment or destiny.

I am however unsure about serendipity, the idea that events come together and cause a greater event which, without the existence of one of the other factors, would not have happened. Serendipity is also a good thing, unlike coincidence, which can fall into either camp. You will never hear anyone say, 'that was an unlucky bit of serendipity', but the term 'unfortunate coincidence' runs rampant across the airwaves.

Incidentally, the word 'serendipity' didn't exist before 1754, when Horace Walpole released it into the wild, where it bred successfully and became a part of our colourful verbal/written countryside.

I always find it odd that words and phrases once never existed – all those things that we say now without even thinking about it, that have become as much a part of us as our ears or our fingers. What did we say before we said 'Brave New World', as Shakespeare did in The Tempest? Where would Aldous Huxley have been without it? What would he have called his book? A quick look in the thesaurus suggests, 'Courageous Updated Society'. I'm not sure that works, although I am willing to bet that, given half a chance, the phrase would trend on Twitter like billy-o (or billio), as these things seem to nowadays.

I digress. This is a bad habit in a writer. Don't do it.

In 1988, I was beginning my training to be a nurse at Wexham Park Hospital in Slough. I was living in a small room in the nurses' quarters at King Edward VII Hospital in Windsor. It was basic – it had a sink, a bed, a chest of drawers and a window. I would still be there now if

a) they hadn't pulled the place down a few years ago and

b) serendipity hadn't walked in.

Prior to that, I had been a porter at Heatherwood Hospital in Ascot. My mother had thrown me out of the house in a fit of pique one day and that was how I ended up living in the nurses' home in Windsor, prior to even becoming a nurse.

I stayed there for the first year of my training. It was convenient. The two hospitals were conjoined, along with Wexham Park Hospital in Slough, to create a sort of NHS Cerberus, the growling bouncer that guarded a special kind of hell. In those days it wasn't like these hideous trusts that we have today, it was just about which health authority you came under and they were all run like potty farms, with the loons in charge.

I had been given a typewriter that the hospital (in Ascot - keep up!) was going to throw away. A friend of mine called Steve, also a porter, had found it on a pile of scrap, stuffed it under his ample jacket and smuggled it to me at the nurses' home.

It was built like the scaffolding that you see on the sides of ancient monuments. To depress a single key required the same pounds per square inch that it takes to jackhammer concrete. It weighed about the same as a very fat three year old and the noise it made actually registered on a sound level meter. We were directly on the flight path to Heathrow; the planes came over so low that you could hear the passengers buckling up. That was nothing in comparison to my Olympia. It was the equivalent of an ungainly tap dancer on a tin tray. It must have annoyed the entire nurses' home.

This, however, was where it all began.

I started with poetry, a few songs, lyrics for a concept album and all the time I had this nugget of an idea sitting in my brain just waiting to be mined, but I couldn't quite dig my way down to it.

Then I met a girl.

For someone who wants to write, this can be good or bad. In my case, it was quite...serendipitous. You see where I'm going with this?

This girl, Sally, who later became my wife, was my drinking companion (along with a chap called Robert) for the next couple of years. Like most students, we drank a lot. I can't remember much of that time. I drank because I was depressed. They drank because they were good at it. My wife is from Barnsley, so it was second nature to her. Being a soft southerner, tea was enough to get me giddy, so when alcohol appeared I was lurching towards and befriending almost all the porcelain I could find.

That is a touch hyperbolic. I just wanted to emphasise how I had been misled by a woman. Writing is like the blues; if you can find a howling dog, a woman and the bottom of a bottle, you're there.

One night, we were drinking again and making generally good banter when my wife laughed. Only, she didn't, she *snorted*. Like a pig. She was mortified but, never being ones to let the opportunity slip, between us we came up with the name of the main character for my first book - Snort Laughter. Upon this precarious rock, *Earthbound* was born.

I haven't stopped writing since.

Serendipity, you see?

So what are the aims of this book?

- To make you aware of the different types of

writing – you are not confined.

- To reinforce those skills you already have. Yes, you do already have some skills.

- To build upon the skills you gain. It's all about practice. There is a thing called muscle memory. If you repeat a movement often enough, your body will remember the action. The brain is the same. It's like weight lifting for those little grey cells. You can become very good at something through repetition. Practice makes perfect.

- To be confident to carry on writing once you put this book down.

- To help others to create. This might seem a bit namby pamby, but it isn't. At the time of writing, I work with students (although summer's here and I don't know if the budget will stretch to next year[1]). I am constantly rewarded by helping them, especially in English, because I am trying to get them to see the relevance and the beauty of language and trying to show them that, through words, they have a voice. That applies to every one of us.

At times, you might think this a little basic. I shall look at some rudimentary writing techniques that I have used with students. It's a starting point. You have to finish it.

I'm not an English teacher; there are far better people out there to do that. Neither is this book about English. This is about writing and whatever happens to be

---

[1] It didn't. I ended up working in a warehouse which, to be honest, is way better.

relevant to it.

In the words of Dirty Harry: 'A man's gotta know his limitations.'

Something Worth Writing

'Either write something worth reading or do something
worth writing.'

Benjamin Franklin

Mr Franklin was a clever guy. He was a great
scientist. He invented terms such as battery, positive,
negative and condenser, all in an electrical sense, and wrote
essays about flatulence (avoidance rather than instigation).
He was a masterful politician who, in one of his quieter
moments, came up with the idea of the flexible urinary
catheter and the Franklin Stove. He was relentless in his
pursuit of discovery and self-improvement. He also had an
enormous sexual appetite. I mention him because,
whatever his motives for such endeavours, he had a need,
a drive, to make his mark in the world, to find his place. I
don't think he did too badly.[2]

It is the same for artists of all types, whether it be
painting, writing, dance or any other art. There is in the
artist an innate need to express and when for some reason
they are unable to do this, they turn inwardly and start to
decompose.

So the first thing I say is: Just Write. Anything.
Anywhere.

À la Pink Floyd, I have a little black book in which
I make my scribblings. It cost £1.40 from The Range.
Bargain. It has such ramblings in there that I don't even
know what most of it means, but there are also substantial
amounts of 'book' in there, pages that have been drafted

---

[2] Thanks to Bill Bryson and *Made in America* for this info. Great book. Great
writer.

and redrafted until I feel able to put them down in a more formal fashion. I also, I might add, use a pencil. One of those mechanical ones. For some reason I cannot scribble in pen. Maybe it's because I have the freedom to erase with a pencil. The notebook also contains the foetal wrigglings of poems and concepts and alternative ways to express the same idea. It has been invaluable. I have also used scrap paper, tissue, the back of my hand, the backs of other books. I even once burst into my daughter's bedroom in just a towel, dripping head to toe in bathwater, to demand a pen and a piece of scrap paper. The only good thing in that story is that she didn't have a friend round at the time.

Needs must as the devil drives.

By the way, there is no obligation to use one of those mechanical pencils. I just happen to like them.

Once this is done though, where do you go? I would not recommend a sixty-year-old Olympia typewriter. My index fingers are bent. I'm sure that it was the Olympia that did that to them.

I wouldn't recommend longhand either, but that is a personal preference. In this era of word processors, I'm not sure that longhand is necessarily a viable option any more. For someone as lazy as me, it's too much like bloody hard work.

If you have invested in a laptop or a PC, I would thoroughly recommend a word processor. They are convenient, flexible, user friendly, save the trouble of transferring from longhand to type and can be linked into so many other programs that it's a wonder our brains work at all.

Here are some suggestions for word processor programs:

- Apache OpenOffice Writer

- LibreOffice Writer
- Wordpad
- Microsoft Word
- AbiWord
- Google Docs

They are all fabulous. I have a friend with whom I wrote the *Praxis* series of books who used Wordpad, while I used Microsoft Word, and it presented no problems. The only discrepancy I came across were certain layout issues, which conflicted with Word, but which were easily resolved.

Let's look at a couple of them.

LibreOffice is a free office suite in the vein of Microsoft Office. This is a review of the software from PC Magazine in August 2015:

- **Pros**
  Open source. Available for Windows, OS X, and Linux. Fast. Powerful. Opens virtually all legacy documents. Improved import and export features.
- **Cons**
  Clunky interface. Confusing menu options. No cloud-based or tablet-based versions.
- **Bottom Line**
  LibreOffice 5.0 provides much of the power of Microsoft Office, but in an outdated and inconsistent interface. Still, it's free and open source, and those who can't or won't use proprietary software won't find anything better.

If you look at the control panel at the top, the toolbar and menu bar, you will see that it has so much in common with Microsoft Word, the standard setter in this field, as to make it difficult to tell them apart.

If you compare this to Microsoft Word,

you'll see how much they have in common.

You can also see, from the varying layouts, bullet points, different indents to paragraphs, fonts, images, that you have an almost inexhaustible number of ways to express yourself.

Both MS Word and LibreOffice come as part of an office suite that offers a degree of compatibility with all the other programs in the suite and therefore ease of access and use. What it really boils down to is whether you want to pay for MS Office (although there are some great student deals out there on Office 365, which even comes with certain brands of mobile phone) or whether you want to go with the open source equivalent.

The thing about Microsoft, whether you like it or not, is that the world deals in everything MS. Not using MS can give some compatibility issues when dealing with others, such as publishers and agents, who often require submissions to be offered up for slaughter in MS Word. Don't blame me; it's the way the world turns.

However, to have such great alternatives as all the others listed here really means that there's no excuse not to have the software, so long as you have the hardware.

If you don't have the hardware, there are pens and paper at The Range[3].

I do have a caveat about word processors though.

They lie. Frequently. They are borderline sociopathic in the tales they tell. They will flip from language to language for no apparent reason. I have written a book in Australian. Really. No matter how often I changed it, it slipped back into the antipodean tongue. I have written other pieces in American.

Now you might think, quite reasonably, that this doesn't matter, English is English. There are *eighteen* choices of English on my version of Word. Each of them in their own way will throw up variables in the same way that a cat throws up hairballs. It is so annoying.

As well as being just annoying though, it matters, because you should be able to trust the software that you are using. Don't. The other more serious problem is that, if you intend to submit your work, there must be a consistency and a correctness to the grammar and spelling. A publisher will reject your work within thirty seconds if you present what is, to them, badly spelled or grammatically poor work. You are responsible for your word processor's action.

Another problem I have noticed frequently is that Word is wrong. It's that simple. It misinterprets sentence structures, it changes spelling when you want the original spelling that you used and it will put in its own grammar or tell you insistently that you are wrong.

But, it is not a human being. It will not be offended if you correct it and it cannot interpret things that you write – it tries to, bless it – but it can only do what it's

---

[3] And other good stationery stores. NB the future is here. Buy a bloody laptop.

programmed to do. So when it throws red across your page in a murderous correctional rampage, don't take its word for it. Double-check it and double-check yourself.

You can add words to its dictionary and you can make it more aware of your foibles, but it is not able to read your mind. Don't be bullied by it. It does not know more than you, it is simply a tool designed to help you achieve.

You have to treat a word processor in much the same way as you do a Tom-Tom[4]. Always read the road signs.

Another very important thing to consider is the environment in which you work.

JK Rowling, a woman whom I greatly admire, is famously known for writing the first Harry Potter book in the Elephant House coffee shop in Edinburgh.

That would drive me absolutely round the bend. I have all the concentration of a kitten. If I went into a coffee shop to write, the only thing I would leave with is a large bill. The traffic outside would distract me, the people inside would distract me, the scraping of chairs and the constant chest clearing of the espresso machines, the jolly chatter of the baristas, that underlying mumble of mutter from the customers who constantly come and go and the smells would all conspire to steal my thoughts.

My ideal environment is silence, a comfortable chair and my computer with all those little accoutrements such as a thesaurus to hand. I cannot work with people around and that includes family.

I have learned my limits. I can concentrate for perhaps an hour and a half at a time and then I need to stop for a while and clear my mind. My back can stand only

---

[4] Yes, I know. There are other machines available to help you become stuck under a low bridge or guide you into a river.

a certain amount of time in the same position before I end up like Quasimodo. My eyes can only put up with a certain amount of computer screen before they begin to feel tired, which in turn affects my concentration.

You will learn your own limitations with time and practice, but they are all important factors to take into account if you wish to put your best into your work.

As a bit of an NB here: let's not forget paper. I have a thesaurus, a dictionary, medical reference books and a wonderful book by Benjamin Zephaniah that contains every rhyming word in the entire universe. Lifesavers, the lot of them.

In The Beginning Was The Word…

There is no such thing as writer's block. I'm not even going to capitalise it. It craves too much.

Hemingway, who had been in the middle of wars, said that the only thing that scared him was a blank sheet of paper. There have been reams written about this mysterious force that empties minds and causes madness. I'm surprised Mulder and Scully didn't come across it. The internet is littered with advice about how to overcome it.

Let's be clear here, there is no such thing as writer's block.

Let's look at the alternatives for this rank disease:

a) A poor working environment – We've just done this. Do not underestimate the importance of your environment. Teachers and academics have been fiddling with the learning environment for years because they understand the importance of psychological and physical comfort. Ergonomics play a massive part in office design.

b) Guilt – Writers do not take themselves seriously and frankly, not many people take them seriously. It just doesn't seem like a 'proper job'. Many actors and artists feel that what they are doing is not work because they enjoy it so much and feel somehow guilty for the rewards they get. Writers are not doctors, nurses, teachers or firemen. They do not save lives. They don't get up in the morning knowing they have to come face to face with someone's scooped out bowel or be steeped in grief. Good. I've done that. It was, to be honest, horrible. We must all tread our own path. We were not all born to be a 'part of the team', to take stress, to work nine to five, to put up with whining managers or internal politics. You know what? That's okay. I've done all those too. They were also horrible.

There is also another kind of guilt and that is bringing yourself into your work. Those who write, especially when they are starting out, tend to put the brakes on because they do not want to share those dark parts of themselves. Let me tell you, dear reader, those are the best parts. Your secret perversions, your wrongs, your desire to kill, your desire to care, your cynicism, your disgust and your love are what are going to bring your book and the characters within to life. You can get away with murder. You can have characters express opinions in a deniable arena – 'no, I don't think that. Those were the thoughts of Jenkins the butler' – and you can purge yourself of some dark, dark meat. It takes a certain amount of self-awareness and honesty to do this, but the rewards are immense, both in terms of what ends up on the page and therapeutically. Writing does me a power of good.

c) Laziness – Don't you deny it. I don't. I am the laziest person alive. I would starve if I didn't have supermarkets (and a wife who was willing to go there on my behalf). There are times when I just don't feel like writing and I procrastinate. Writer's block is procrastination *par excellence*. Just write. Anything. Get a piece of paper or turn on the PC/laptop and get some words down. Try to string them into a sentence. It doesn't have to mean anything or be relevant. Pick a word out of a dictionary and write everything you can think of about that word. Do anything to stimulate the process. You are the only one who can do this. This is a lonely path that you tread. It's your responsibility, no one else's.

d) Lack of knowledge – Really? *Really*? I am

surrounded by books, all of which I have read. I have consumed words. I watch documentaries on TV. I watch programs on YouTube. I (yes, it's a verb) Google. There is nothing about which you cannot find information.

I wrote *A Beginner's Guide to the Wars of the Roses*. I love history and found it to be a fascinating subject. I still do. I cross-referenced the thirty or so books that I had read and did some research on the internet along with that. I didn't believe a word I was told, not even in the books. Every fact was double and triple checked. It was hard, engrossing and rewarding work. As far as lack of knowledge goes, you only have yourself to blame I'm afraid. Open your horizons. Broaden your knowledge. If you're not writing, read.

e) Intimidation – I agree with Hemingway to some extent. A blank page is a horrific thing. It is a very intimidating thing. I hate starting a new book because I know how much work is ahead of me, how much research, how much imagination, how much it will drag from me on a personal level, the constant pressure of making each word within each sentence on each page in each chapter count.

People who read what you have written are unforgiving. If they don't like the first page, they won't buy the book. If they didn't like the last book, they won't buy the next one. This is assuming that you can get someone to pick your book up in the first place.

The only thing I can do is set my own standards and write for myself. There is always the temptation to think that you will exclude or offend some part of your audience, but often the exclusion of one means the inclusion of another and that offence can very often be what simulates the reader to carry on. Everybody likes a good argument.

We are all intimidated by many things — lack of knowledge, lack of skill, lack of talent, fear of rejection, fear of acceptance, the fact that the world has seven and a half billion people in it and not everyone will like your book, the fact that you might fail. It comes with the territory, I'm sorry to say.

I write for myself. I write because I have an idea that I need to express and there is no way that I can stop it seeping from my pores. I love the idea that I can get down on paper something that has been gnawing at me for months, maybe years.

Intimidation subsides with practice. All of these problems do.

The list could go on. These are just some of the things that *I* have felt. What about you? You might have a whole bunch of other reasons. Maybe you should write a list. On a blank page. Who knows where it might lead?

Make no mistake; what a writer does is valuable. Writing has changed the world. It has empowered the poor and the illiterate and the oppressed. It has spread messages of hope where previously none existed. It has sparked revolutions and brought about peace. It has freed us from our own bonds. It certainly liberates me in a way that nothing else I do does.

PART TWO: PROSE

Prose – What Is It?

> The ordinary form of spoken or written language, without metrical structure, as distinguished by poetry or verse.

Dictionary.com

Prose is often described as 'plain or dull writing'...hmmm!

Prose is merely a combination of words, grammar and ideas. It is the representation (in our case written) of a person's thoughts, values, ideas, wishes, lies, dreams, perceptions, experience etc. There is no right and wrong.

There are, however, sold and unsold.

It is not poetry or rhyming verse or an article for a magazine, although they have a lot in common.

So How Do You Write Prose?

The truth? However you want. Don't write for other people. You will not please all of the people all of the time and you will drown in opinions.

Write for yourself. Appraise your own work critically, but realistically. If you want to write for a particular market, does what you have written really reach that target? If you want to write a love scene, has it actually turned out to be little more than a squelchy quickie or has it torn out your heart? Either may be too much or too little.

There are certain boundaries that you need to apply. Some people call them rules, but I think that's a bit heavy-handed. Applying rules can petrify free thought and I would rather people were able to get their ideas down than be hesitant because of a bunch of rules.

However (sorry), I'm going to show you some

rules that two great writers have shared. They are available freely on the internet, along with a million other sets of rules and opinions, but I like these for two reasons: they are written by established authors who each come at writing with a different approach, they have experience to offer and I pretty much agree with them.

The two authors are George Orwell, he of *Animal Farm* etc and Elmore Leonard, he of *Rum Punch* etc.

Let's start with Mr Orwell.

George Orwell's 5 Rules for Effective Writing

1. Never use a metaphor, simile, or other figure of speech which you are used to seeing in print.

Clichés. They are so convenient. They say what you want to say wrapped up in a nice little, easily disposed of bundle. Well, an owl pellet is an easily disposed of bundle too and you don't want to see too many of those. The thing is, clichés have become clichés because they are overused. They have lost their impact because they have become such a common part of everyday communication. They no longer stand out in a sentence. A metaphor or a simile is there to bring the reader's attention to something, make them stop and think or laugh or go 'Oh, yeah'.

2. Never use a long word where a short one will do.

KISS. Keep It Simple Stupid.

I am so guilty of this crime. I like words and I like new words and I think other people should like my new words. I'm wrong. Other people should understand my words and if I use words that people don't understand or I litter my work with such things, people will lose interest. Sure, every once in a while, stretch yourself and stretch your reader, but not on the rack.

3. If it is possible to cut a word out, always cut it out.

Short sentences. I find if I read a long sentence, as I often do with students, I lose my breath, because we read as we talk. If we have to read a long sentence, we a) lose the meaning and b) begin to feel physically uncomfortable.

The same applies to paragraphs and chapters. One author I was reading about said that she thought it was a good idea to keep chapters at ten pages or less. I have taken that on board. It helps me focus. Here are some phrases that have unnecessary words and that really, really annoy me:

Free gift – what other kind of gift is there?
Almost exactly – It's either exactly or it isn't.
Almost unique – This is impossible.

Very or quite similar – There is no degree of similarity. It's either similar or it isn't.

Envy/Jealousy – They are not the same. Jealousy is about emotions. Envy is about possession of objects or more abstract concepts, but not emotions.

There are so many of these, I could scream. I do actually, especially at the TV.

You can get rid of fifty percent of these words.

4. Never use the passive where you can use the active.

The man was bitten by the dog (passive). The dog bit the man (active). The active is better because it's shorter and more forceful.

In relation to number 3, this is a good point. It creates shorter sentences and has more impact.

A word of warning. MS Word is constantly prattling on at me about using the passive. It's not always right, so don't change something just because your word processor says so. It is however a good way to re-examine your work and perhaps rephrase things.

I admit to finding this difficult and need to practice it more.

5. **Never use a foreign phrase, a scientific word, or a jargon word if you can think of an everyday English equivalent.**

This is interesting. We are now in a more jargonistic (I have just invented that word, I think) age and so much of what we read has been imported into everyday language via technology. It has happened quickly too. Be aware of this because by being too jargonistic (I like it) it is very easy to exclude others.

The other thing to be aware of is using dialect. This is for two main reasons: one is that the reader might not understand it and two is that it can cause offence.

One example of this is Irvine Welsh, who likes to write in a Scottish dialect. This from *Trainspotting:*

> Anywey, this time ah've prepared. A month's rent in advance oan this big, bare room overlooking the Links. Too many bastards ken ma Montgomery Street

address. Cash oan the nail! Partin wi that poppy wis the hardest bit. The easiest wis ma last shot, taken in ma left airm this morning.

Now, this adds authenticity and gives the reader that valuable sense of time and place. It's very involving. There is a danger though that this might exclude others. He might lose sales because people simply cannot be arsed to trawl their way through a bag of dialect.

Offence through ignorance or socially accepted attitudes, even when used to add that sense of time and place, is a risky business.

I don't like to criticise Ian Fleming, but there were times when his attitude to blacks had that awful, colonial, superior tone that makes me cringe.

He's an extract from one of his biggest culprits, *Live and Let Die*:

The man's voice suddenly sharpened. 'Wha' dat Birdie he mean tuh yuh, hey?' he asked suspiciously. 'Terzackly,' he paused to let the big word sink in, 'perzackly wha' goes 'tween yuh 'n dat lowdown ornery wuthless Nigguh? Yuh sleepin' wid him mebbe? Guess Ah gotta study 'bout dat little situayshun 'tween yuh an' Birdie Johnson. Mebbe git mahself a betterer gal. Ah jist don' lak gals which runs off ever' which way when Ah jist happen be busticated tem-poraneously. Yesmam. Ah gotta study 'bout dat little situayshun.' He paused threateningly. 'Sure have,' he added.

Madness! Utter madness! I'm certain that nobody would write like this today, but it highlights a couple of things of which we still need to be aware. One is that the script is practically unreadable. It takes so much effort to get through it that there is no reward great enough. The second is that it is racist and offensive. It marks blacks out as illiterate and as a source of ridicule. This paragraph and a couple of the paragraphs around it could easily have been removed with absolutely no effect on the narrative.

Neither am I however in favour of butchering work. We should not change it now in light of the political changes though which we have gone. It must however make us aware.

So should we, as writers, use the word 'nigger'? No, not in the normal way of things, but I have done and I will explain why. I was writing a short story about racism and the lynching of a black man. He was referred to as a 'nigger'.

> 'Now, I know that there was a lawman called Deputy Stevens. I also know that it was Deputy Stevens who bumped Lucy on the head for no good reason and called him nigger-shit.'

From *Killer* – Chris Bradbury

This said something about the man who used that word towards a black man. It highlighted his prejudices, his upbringing, the social norms in that part of the world. It was an essential part of the make-up of the tale. I used it three times in that story and in an appropriate context and was very clear about the context in which it was used.

Now, I live in Barnsley, but am not from Barnsley.

I am a southerner, as I am frequently reminded, because I have a weird accent.

If I were writing about Barnsley and used a common phrase such as,

'‘e were built like a brick shit'ouse.’

it would be fine because that is the way they speak. However, if I let it slip into parody as Fleming did, then they have an absolute right to complain.

The final point on this is about the use of foreign words when an English one will do. It's quite right. It can come across as pretentious, snobby and condescending (and rather jejune – sorry, I just had to). It can also exclude part of your readership. Use these only when it is necessary. Just ask yourself, each time you use a long, over-complicated foreign word, 'How much money had that just lost me?'. You'll soon stop.

Elmore Leonard's 10 Rules For Writing

1) Never open a book with weather.

Why? Cliché. We've been through this. Also, it leads onto the next one.

2) Avoid prologues.

Procrastination.
Get to the point. Start with Chapter One.
This is now where I admit to using a prologue. I needed it as a scene setter, many years previous to the actual events in the story, in *Praxis*.
Was I right to do so? It was right for me and it was

discussed with my writing partner, so it wasn't a snap decision. In the end, I'm comfortable with it. Generally, I don't use them.

3) Never use a verb other than 'said' to carry dialogue.

This, I love. I'm going to show you a bit of Leonard's writing.

Raylan turned the knob to let the water run out, lowering it around Angel, his belly becoming an island in the tub of ice water, blood showing in two places on the island.

"He had something done to him," Raylan said. "He's got like staples closing up what look like wounds. Or was he operated on?"

"Somebody shot him," Tim said.

"I don't think so," Raylan said, staring at the two incisions stapled closed.

Rachel said, "That's how they did my mother last year, at UK Medical. Made one entry below the ribs and the other under her belly button. I asked her why they did it there 'stead of around through her back."

Tim said, "You gonna tell us what the operation was?"

"They took out her kidneys," Rachel said. "Both of 'em, and she got an almost new pair the same day, from a child who'd drowned."

They wrapped Angel in a blanket, carried him into the bedroom and laid him on the spread, the man shuddering, trying to breathe. His eyes closed he said to Raylan staring at him, "What happen to me?"

"You're here makin' a deal?"

<u>Angel hesitated</u>. "Two guys I know, growers. We have a drink—"

"And you end up in the tub," <u>Raylan said.</u> "How much you pay them?"

From *Raylan* – Elmore Leonard

If you look at the underlined parts, you will see what Leonard was saying.

The reason I like this so much is that he allows the characters to speak with only the tiniest amount of description around the dialogue. The characters' words have impact. We already know the characters' attitudes, so now they can tell their tale and we can listen to them without being interrupted by wandering adverbs.

I consciously try to do this. I'm not always successful, but it does make for a snappier read, more satisfactory prose and livelier speech.

4) Never use an adverb to modify the verb 'said'…he admonished gravely.

As above. I confess, I do sometimes use adverbs to modify a verb. I feel shame.

5) Keep your exclamation points under control. You are allowed no more than two or three per 100,000 words of prose.[5]

---

[5] From the man himself.

If you have set the context up correctly, you should not need an exclamation mark to indicate anything.

6) Never use the words 'suddenly' or 'all hell broke loose'.

Be more inventive. Events are rarely sudden, especially in books. It also suggests a lack of imagination on the writer's part. On top of this, the reader can feel a little cheated if they are not in on the secret and they will love it if you do share.

7) Use regional dialect, patois, sparingly.

For the reasons mentioned in Number 5 of Mr Orwell's section.

8) Avoid detailed descriptions of characters.

I don't necessarily agree with this. Leonard is famous for defining a female character as American. That was it. He wanted the reader to paint their own picture.
Ian Fleming went the other way.
I think Fleming went a little too far sometimes and it did hold up the narrative, but on the other hand, it involved the reader.
You have to make your own choice
.

9) Don't go into great detail describing places and things.

As above really. It's sometimes nice to take a bit of time out, as a reader, to enjoy the scenery. But don't ruin the narrative. Don't let the pacing suffer.

10) Try to leave out the part that readers tend to skip.

This is one of those tips that is obvious after you think about it. We all skip parts when we read. It might be the description of a dress, a piece of furniture, how the flight went, the taste of the sea bass on the plane.

There is one author who does the most fantastic research into his history books and they make an absorbing read, but once in a while he goes all soft and lovey-dovey on me and feels the need to talk about the theatre of the time or the artists influenced by the social upheaval of the time. I read those bits lightly. Very lightly.

Lost in Da Forest

We can be eaten by techniques and forget what we have inside of us.

Eric Cantona

My wife loves Eric Cantona. This is why he is here. That and the fact that what he says is very true.

Writing is full of snobbery. It is full of 'should do this' and 'should do that' and I think this inhibits people. Sometimes it even prevents people writing altogether and that is a terrible thing.

I'm not one to follow rules too tightly. I once said to a student that I didn't care if his spellings were wrong, it was his ideas I wanted. We could look at the spellings later. I was told off by the boss for this. It was worth it. He vomited ideas out that day because he was able to focus on what mattered. He had permission, freedom and focus.

There are a couple of techniques however, that I believe really do help improve written work.

One of them is called the DAFOREST technique, which looks at some simple yet effective ways to grab the reader's attention. The other technique, called THE MOIST PEARS (I kid you not) looks at poetry techniques and we will visit those later. I wasn't taught these at school. I wish I had been. They prise open doors and let you into little secrets that can turn sentences and paragraphs into wonders of the world.

I agree with Eric, despite my wife's dreamy infidelity. Don't lose your heart among all the clever tricks.

DA FOREST

D - Direct address
A - Alliteration
F - Facts
O - Opinions
R - Rhetorical questions/Repetition
E - Emotive language
S - Statistics/Structure
T - Rule of three/Triplets

DAFOREST is a mnemonic to help students to remember language techniques or persuasive language.

I'll go through the acronym letter by letter. It's a bit like *Do-Re-Mi* from *The Sound of Music*, but I like that song. There is a DAFOREST song on YouTube if you want to hear it. It will make you want to kill someone, but it's there if you want it.

This might seem a little basic and 'back to school' but, if you do want to write successfully, then it is the basics that matter. Trust me.

So, let's go through DAFOREST. As you read, if you have already written something, try to apply it to what you have already done. See if there are any tweaks you can apply.

D – Direct Address.

This is intended to engage the reader, to make them feel as if they want to read further and that, by being addressed directly, the text is relevant to them.

It involves the use of You, I, etc. It can also be through the use of a proper noun (name), which is also known as the 'noun of address' e.g. Chris, as in, 'Chris, have a bath. You smell.' 'Chris' is the noun of address.

You are (see what I did there?) addressing the reader directly. Even a chair can become the noun of address. If you stub your toe on the chair, you curse the chair. We've all done it. If you haven't, your time will come.

Some dispute that 'I' is a form of direct address. This can be brought up with relevance to books. This book, an instructional book, uses a lot of 'you's and 'I's. This helps me, the writer, relate to you, the reader. It's like breaking the fourth wall in movies. Do you remember when Oliver Hardy would stare into the camera? When Thomas Magnum from *Magnum PI* would do the same? When Benedict Cumberbatch recently did it as Richard III in the BBC's Hollow Crown series? It is a very effective way of creating intimacy with the observer or reader and of bringing them into the subject. It is inclusion rather that unintentional exclusion.

The same could be said for writing in the first person in fiction. There is an implied sharing when the writer says 'I'. If you look at *The Catcher in the Rye* or *To Kill a Mockingbird,* you will see that they are written in the first person. It is as if the writer is letting you, and just you, into a secret. It's not just a telling; it's a *sharing.*

Look at *Fifty Shades of Grey*! OMG! I'm not sure how effective that would have been in third person, but written in the first person, it lends such an intimacy and gives such *permission* to the reader, both in imagination and in actuality, that it is almost a confidential letter to a friend. You are within the story, not observing it from the outside.

The argument for third person is that it gives the reader (and the writer) the distance, the objectivity, which is required for them to enjoy the different strands of a tale, layered by multiple characters, within what is often a slightly more convoluted plot, mainly because you are following more than one character.

This does not mean to say that the first person plot cannot offer complexity; it is just more difficult to credibly write the story without the main character being there? How can they have known what is going on elsewhere if they were not there? To recount it second-hand, as in hearsay, is clumsy and lacks credibility within this context. In third person, you can switch between protagonist and antagonist almost at will without the restrictions imposed by the usage of the first person.

A – Alliteration.

Alliteration is the use of two words in a row (or close by each other) that begin with the same letter. I will give you an example of this from a short story of mine called *Wintergreen*.

'The coach rattled across the rutted road.'

I could have said something like:

'The coach bumped its way along the pot-holed track.'

The secret to the alliteration is that it makes it easier to read, it is more pleasing to the tongue and it is less guttural. The reader's eyes skim over it more easily. It is instantly more memorable and produces the same images to the reader as the alternative sentence, but those images are more concrete, have greater impact. Even though the word 'rattled' is not next to the other two 'r' words, 'rutted' and 'road', it still has an impact because of the rhythm of the sentence and its proximity to the other words.

To stray slightly into poetry territory, Carol Anne Duffy uses it to great effect in *Medusa*, the fine modern poem about exclusion and love and jealousy and isolation.

> 'My <u>b</u>ride's <u>b</u>reath soured, stank
> in the grey <u>b</u>ags of my lungs.'

By using this alliteration, she draws the reader's attention to those two words and makes you ask, 'why has she mentioned 'bride's breath?'' It forces the reader to search for depth of meaning by focusing upon them with something as simple as alliteration. Even the word 'bag' in the next line jumps out at the reader because of the previous alliteration and presents further questions to the reader.

F – Facts.

Do not think that you can get away from these, even in sci-fi. If you omit one, if you get one wrong, if you make one up, it will haunt you forever.

Facts are about maintaining the character's, the book's and the writer's credibility. They are about sustaining the reader's belief so that a scenario, however unlikely, can be carried through successfully to its conclusion.

There are obvious times when you need facts. Now, for example. It would serve neither of us any purpose to give you lies. You wouldn't trust me again and my book sales would suffer through poor reviews and word of mouth. Your writing would suffer because of me.

When writing *The Beginner's Guide to the Wars of the Roses*, facts were vital, so all sources needed to be checked and checked again.

There was a moment, in another book, when I went a little wild, which I probably shouldn't confess, but will because it has a point to make.

I was writing a book called *Condition of Life: The Poetic Confessions of a Grumpy Old Man*. This combined the elements of poetry and biography. I told the stories of the poems and related them to my life, past and present. It was fun, unnerving, a little intimidating due to the honesty required and a very interesting project to complete.

I was feeling a little flippant one day and wrote something down about fruit-eaters. I don't like fruit. I'm never sure about people who do eat fruit. Anyway, I made a slightly wild but genuinely felt statement about fruit-eaters and their personalities. Upon reflection, reason and a smidgen of guilt overtook me and I thought, you can't write that, it's unfair, unbalanced and unproven. So I sought to prove it by means of the internet. Lo and behold, there was a piece of research linking fruit eating and personality. I used it. Mostly to annoy fruit-eaters, or frugivores as they are known in their habitats – on bicycles, running tracks, in gyms etc.

The point is that the research is out there, especially now, with all this wonderful technology. Find your facts, don't get them wrong and make your readers trust you. Even frugivores.

That's the non-fiction bit done, but don't think you don't need to research fiction. Especially sci-fi. If you get on the wrong side of a sci-fi nut, you'll never hear the end of it.

I have written three books in the *Praxis* series with my friend Ian Makinson. It had never occurred to me to write sci-fi until Ian invited me to join him. I had always thought of it as something for those who...well...for weirdos. I stand by that. Ian's weird. He knows all there is to know about Dr Who and Warhammer. Ask him where a semi-colon goes and he logs himself off and needs rebooting, but in his field, he's a master.

I thought that you could get away with anything in sci-fi. I was so wrong. The amount of times he said to me that something simply was not possible (while suppressing his geek laugh), was ridiculous, but he knew his stuff and I had to be guided by him.

In another book, *The Ashes of an Oak*, I had decided to place my protagonist, a New York police detective, in 1970s Brooklyn.

Easy, you would think.

I had to research:

- New York, specifically Brooklyn, in 1970
- Speech patterns
- Police procedure of the time
- Forensics of the time
- The hierarchy of an American police precinct in 1970
- The cars of the time
- Anatomy - the decomposition of the body, the effects of injuries, brain tumours
- Which cigarettes were around at the time
- When the laws against smoking in hospitals and the workplace came into force in the USA
- Frank Sinatra
- The weather for the time that I'm writing about – if you think this is going too far, I have read an analysis of Ian Fleming's James Bond books that looks at the *phases*

of the moon at the time of the events in which Bond is involved.[6] It is both fascinating and scary.

- A calendar to ensure that I matched date and day.
- Drinks of the time
- Food of the time
- Events of the time - for example, there had been a bad fire in Pine Street, Brooklyn, in March of that year. It added a touch of authenticity.

It all takes time, patience and a determination to not be caught out by a stranger on the other side of the world. It is worth it, for two reasons. One is that whatever you put down on paper and publish, will be correct. The other reason, which I enjoy tremendously, is that you learn stuff, all the time. That's the great thing about working with students because, as you help them learn, so you learn along with them. In this case, you are the student. It makes *Eggheads* more bearable anyway.

O – Opinions.

In fiction, opinions are expressed through the characters. Readers do not like to be lectured. People who read are intelligent enough to form their own opinions. Let those opinions be about your characters, not about you. Part of the reason that I didn't like the film *Avatar* is because for the first half, I felt like I was being preached to about the environment. It put me off.

---

[6] *Ian Fleming's James Bond: Annotations and Chronologies for Ian Fleming's Bond Stories* - John Griswold - 2005

That's not to say that the author's personality and beliefs do not creep out through the character.

Let's use James Bond as an example.

Fleming made no secret of his likes and dislikes through Bond. His women, the ones that Bond liked, always had short, unpolished fingernails. They often wore a two-inch black belt around their waist. They often wore a choker. They wore sensible flat shoes. Their backside always protruded 'like a boy's' – this is not any homosexual reference, it is to do with the vitality and fitness of the individual.

Bond is famous for his pernickety attitude to food. Fleming too had his preferences. He moved in wealthy, powerful circles and knew a good champagne from a bad.

There is also a rather right-wing attitude to Bond, but also a philosophical bent, a self-awareness, which made him aware that he was a disposable tool. There always seemed to be an underlying unhappiness in Bond. Fleming always appeared to be second best to his brother, Peter and, like Bond, Ian Fleming had done military service. He brought his knowledge of the craft to Bond.

All this made Bond a fascinating, complex character, much underrated in this fella's opinion. The important thing to remember is though, that Fleming never gave out *his* opinions, only his character's. He was aware, as any writer should be, that the public does not want to know the man or woman *behind* the words, they want to know the characters *within* the words.

It's different in non-fiction. In non-fiction, you could class opinion as interpretation. It is important not to show bias or prejudice. In non-fiction, the reader wants a presentation of the facts, hopefully backed up by research. Should the author then put a case forward, based on the evidence, then this could be classed as interpretation and is acceptable to most readers.

In *A Beginner's Guide to the Wars of the Roses*, I inevitably have to talk about the fabulously controversial Richard III. Our history is littered with bias towards and against this man, so I had to try and present a balanced argument based upon the evidence available to me.

> 'This was the dichotomy of Richard of Gloucester and Richard III. It was as if he had had some sort of dark epiphany after the death of his brother, Edward IV.
>
> Within the context of the times, some of his behaviour wasn't unusual. Certainly, Henry VII appeared to behave just as badly, if not worse, than Richard in achieving his own ends and thought nothing of using judicial murder to further his own ends. The same could be applied to Edward IV, but history has been so much kinder to them, largely due to the skilful implementation of Tudor propaganda, right up to modern times.'

What I presented here were reasons why Richard III had a bad press. I do not say that it was unjustified, but I try to put Richard within the context of his times, to let people know that our modern perceptions come with baggage that prejudices our opinions of the past.

The paragraphs around this quote were backed up by similar jousting, neither falling on one side nor the other, but presenting a cogent, rational argument for each.

Never let your emotions get in the way of your writing. The reader doesn't care for your personal opinion. The reader wants to be able to form their own opinion from what is on offer. Your book will not be the only one available on the subject.

The same goes for fiction. If your last paragraph of the book leaves you in tears, for God's sake go back to it once you've stopped blubbing. It might well be that you have invoked the God of Mawkish Soppiness in order to simply get a reaction, not from the reader, but from yourself.

R – Rhetorical Questions
Repetition

These are great though, aren't they, Ted?[7]

I miss Craggy Island. It gave us all those rhetorical questions from Dougal.

A **rhetorical question** is a question that you ask without expecting an answer.

Do they help in writing? (sorry, but I had to ask). Yes and no. There was one writer, and I can't for the life of me remember his/her name, who despised them. They believed that the writer, particularly in fiction, was trying to get the reader to do his work for them or that they were basically doing their dirty washing in public. There should, they felt, be no need for rhetorical questions because decent planning should make them unnecessary.

To an extent, I agree. It is easier to stick in a question than to expound upon a point. It can be a bit lazy.

However, I also think that it is a way to offer the reader a summary of events, a moment to catch up, to take a look at unanswered questions. It involves the reader, almost asks their opinion and drags them along in the guessing game, maybe even perks their attention up a bit.

---

[7] Please say we all remember *Father Ted.*

The argument to that is that your writing should be so good that they do not need perking up.

However, there are times when rhetorical questions are entirely justified. If they can highlight important points or point out to society its prejudices or be used as emotive language, where they not only induce a reaction in the reader, but they also make the reader question their own values.

Here is a good example that speaks of the era, the society and the character within the play:

> 'I am a Jew. Hath not a Jew eyes? Hath not a Jew hands, organs, dimensions, senses, affections, passions; fed with the same food, hurt with the same weapons, subject to the same diseases,
> heal'd by the same means, warm'd and cool'd by the same winter and summer, as a Christian is?
> If you prick us, do we not bleed? If you tickle us, do we not laugh? If you poison us, do we not die?
> And if you wrong us, do we not revenge? If we are like you in the rest, we will resemble you in that.'

William Shakespeare - *The Merchant Of Venice Act 3, scene 1*

I would take issue with anyone who says that these rhetorical questions are too much or unnecessary. I confess, I've only seen the Al Pacino version of this, but this is his moment and he delivers it beautifully.

So, my advice? (sorry). Use it sparingly, to

maximum effect and don't patronise the reader.

Repetition is one of those tricks that makes the words stick in the reader's mind and bring impact to those words. It can not only drill something into the reader's skull, but it can say a lot about a character and their situation.

Here's one of mine, from *The Stilling of the Heart*:

> 'And he <u>hated</u>. He <u>hated</u> with passion. He <u>hated</u> blacks, Chinese, Asians and those of mixed race. He <u>hated</u> single mothers and those with AIDS. He <u>hated</u> the liberals and the socialists. He <u>hated</u> government and the opposition. He <u>hated</u> gays and lesbians, except as a form of entertainment. He <u>hated</u> those who were poor and those who had more than he did. He <u>hated</u> women with opinions and men with balls. He <u>hated</u> the quiet and the shy and the outcasts and the afraid. He <u>hated</u> the police and the criminals. He <u>hated</u> the laws that protected the weak and he <u>hated</u> the laws that protected the strong.'

The use of the word 'hated' says more than just about what he hated. It tells the reader about the man, about his prejudices, about his life balance, about his state of happiness and his insecurities. It indicates to the reader that this might not be a good man. In a wider context, it lets the reader know of the situation in which the protagonist finds himself, the hill that he has to climb when confronted by this man on a daily basis. It helps the reader empathise. It reminds the reader of someone they know. It makes the reader feel something – anger, helplessness, dislike – but it does what all art should do, it pricks at the emotions.

The importance with repetition is to keep it simple. Keep the syllable count down. It will present its own rhythm, in the same way that alliteration does, and worm its way into the consciousness of the reader.

It's also good to use in speech. Repetition can reinforce the characters mood:

> 'I'm happy, I tell you. Happy, happy, happy.'

Or:

> 'I can't do this anymore. I can't. I can't. I can't.'

From these simple words, you can understand the prevailing mood of the moment, the lightness or heaviness not only of the character, but the context in which they say the words. They are unlikely to declare their happiness repeatedly in front of a firing squad.

Once again, like most of these techniques, repetition should be used sparingly. It must represent the moment and allow that moment to have greatest impact. If you use it too often, the impact will fade and the reader might well become immune to the effect and bored.

E – Emotive language

Writers use emotive language in order to have a greater emotional impact on their readers.

It could be argued that the point of all art is to induce an emotional response. Paintings through history have often had hidden meanings intended to convey a message or generate a reaction. Certainly poetry, especially if you read any of the nineteenth century romantics, is there to elicit an emotional response via an intellectual route. The reason the nineteenth century romantics don't work for me is that they wore their heart too much on their sleeve. I prefer subtlety, a carefully measured manipulation (for that is what it is) taken by such as Seamus Heaney.

> I stumbled in his hob-nailed wake,
> Fell sometimes on the polished sod;
> Sometimes he rode me on his back
> Dipping and rising to his plod.
>
> I wanted to grow up and plough,
> To close one eye, stiffen my arm.
> All I ever did was follow
> In his broad shadow round the farm.
>
> I was a nuisance, tripping, falling,
> Yapping always. But today
> It is my father who keeps stumbling
> Behind me, and will not go away.

Seamus Heaney - *Follower*

This is a tremendously powerful and clever piece of writing. Heaney offers you emotion if you want it, but he also lends an almost documentary feel to it. It will mean a lot to those of us with parents who have dementia. To those who don't, it might open the reader to new perceptions.

What Heaney does not do is descend into sentimentality in an attempt to manipulate the reader. He gives the reader freedom of interpretation. Don't get me wrong; all writers in all forms manipulate, the trick is to not let the reader know that they are being manipulated. The whole ride should be a pleasant experience, not a boneshaker.

This applies to fiction and scriptwriting. Those awful movies you see on the True Entertainment channel are deliberately, overtly manipulative and do not leave it to the intelligence of the viewer to interpret.

It doesn't make them wrong. God knows, Mills and Boon didn't do too badly with a solid, predictable and intentionally emotive plot with the language to match it; it just depends upon the market that you want to aim for.

In non-fiction, there is really no place for emotive language. Readers buy books about history or car maintenance to learn, not to cry. If the subject matter is enough to induce tears, don't let that be the author's fault. (I did once buy a Hayne's Manual for a Nissan Almera. I cried for weeks. Not their fault. I have the DIY skills of a lemur.)

Stephen E Ambrose, author of *Band of Brothers,* one among many fine works, was very good at this. He managed to find a fine balance between detachment and emotion; he came close a few times to crossing the line, but his research was always impeccable, which lent him authority and gravity, and he always managed to remain objective enough to allow the situation, the context, to evoke emotions in the reader, rather than his words.

S – Statistics
Structure

Statistics are facts with numbers. That's it. 95% of people know that.

Structure is an incredibly important part of all writing. Take a look at the images of pages below:

'Where exactly?' Tassin pointed to his side. 'Here.' Dr Gilmour nodded sagely. 'Uhuh.' He tapped something into the computer. His fingers moved like cockroaches across a kitchen surface. 'Let's take a peek, shall we? Why don't you pop your top off and jump onto the couch?' Tassin reluctantly popped his top off and jumped onto the couch. The couch had a layer of tissue paper upon it. He felt it crinkle under his back and the creases on his skin. He wanted to get up and straighten it. Dr Gilmour came over. He held his hands together, cradled like surgical instruments and then held them above Tassin's abdomen as if it was part of a ritual. 'I'm just going to prod about a bit,' he said. Tassin felt himself tighten. Dr Gilmour put his hands, which were dry and warm, upon Tassin's belly. He found the spot immediately, then moved on more generally over the abdomen. 'Do you smoke?' 'Yes.' 'Do you drink?' 'Yes.' 'How much?' 'As much as I can afford.' Dr Gilmour looked at Tassin and smiled, then realised that he wasn't joking. 'Roughly?' Tassin frowned. 'A bottle a day. Sometimes more.' 'Of...?' 'Wine. Red. Merlot.' Dr Gilmour peffed a laugh. 'I'm not concerned with the grape, Mr Tassin. Only the amount.' He stopped his prodding and indicated to Tassin to put his clothes back on. 'That's quite a lot.' 'I enjoy it,' said Tassin by way of an excuse. It sounded pathetic. 'Weight loss?' Tassin shrugged. 'A few pounds. No appetite.' 'Do you work?' 'Yes.' 'At what?' 'I deliver frozen food.' 'Do you get any back pain?' 'Some.' Dr Gilmour looked at Tassin's eyes. He pursed his lips and then returned behind his desk. His

bonus. 'Where exactly?'

Tassin pointed to his side. 'Here.'

Dr Gilmour nodded sagely. 'Uhuh.' He tapped something into the computer. His fingers moved like cockroaches across a kitchen surface. 'Let's take a peek, shall we? Why don't you pop your top off and jump onto the couch?'

Tassin reluctantly popped his top off and jumped onto the couch. The couch had a layer of tissue paper upon it. He felt it crinkle under his back and the creases on his skin. He wanted to get up and straighten it.

Dr Gilmour came over. He held his hands together, cradled like surgical instruments and then held them above Tassin's abdomen as if it was part of a ritual.

'I'm just going to prod about a bit,' he said.

Tassin felt himself tighten.

Dr Gilmour put his hands, which were dry and warm, moved immediately, then moved on more generally over the abdomen.

'Do you smoke?'

'Yes.'

'Do you drink?'

'Yes.'

'How much?'

'As much as I can afford.'

Dr Gilmour looked at Tassin and smiled, then realised that he wasn't joking. 'Roughly?'

Tassin frowned. 'A bottle a day. Sometimes

Forget the content. Which of these would you rather read? (this is not a rhetorical question).

I'm willing to bet that, if you were honest, your first instincts would be to go for the one on the right, with the paragraphs, the clear structure, the more attractive silhouette.

Imagine this being a piece of fiction (it is actually) with speech - plot revolving, essential speech - and you had to pick it out from the crowd of ants on the left. I don't know about you, but I'd put it down and look for another book.

Reading should be easy, not necessarily intellectually, but aesthetically. Don't make it difficult for the reader. Much like being comfortable when writing, the reader needs to be comfortable when reading and, as the PC/laptop is important to the writer, so is the book and its layout to the reader.

But it's not just important aesthetically. It is vital to the understanding of the piece. We shall see in the poetry section how vital structure is, especially when using something such as enjambment. Punctuation, paragraphs, those gaps in between (much like the spaces between the notes in music) can alter meaning and interpretation and potentially mislead a reader. At worst, it can drive the reader away.

This is the visual aspect of it.

There is also the *internal* structure to consider and this comes with the planning. There is the basic beginning, middle and end to consider, but there is also that pathway to consider, down which to lead the reader from beginning to end.

If you write a piece for example, as I did, on the Wars of the Roses, I had to structure it quite carefully. I had to consider the chronology of the wars. I didn't want to keep time hopping and confuse the reader – it was aimed at the beginner and it is a very complex subject – but I also wanted to ensure that the whys and wherefores were answered, such as the causes of the wars. I also had to consider the peripheries that were relevant, such as the money of the time (the reader had to somehow relate yesterday's values to today's in order to appreciate the context), the significant dates, the personalities and the battles. I had to present them in such a way that the reader could associate them with each other in order to get an overall view and yet at the same time take them in as an individual element of the piece.

Sentences and paragraphs are an essential part of

these processes. They please the eye and they also help to segregate and make sense of the flood of text.

In fiction, you need to start, once again, with the basics and this will be:

    a) Set-up
    b) Confrontation
    c) Resolution

Or

    d) Beginning
    e) Middle
    f) End

If you can start with these, not just in your head, but also in black and white, on paper or word processor, then you can move on to filling the gaps in between.

Don't be afraid of the word 'confrontation'. All art is confrontation. The poet Simon Armitage uses confrontation, often between just two people, such as in *Clown Punk*, to ignite emotions in the reader. Shakespeare, in all his work, used confrontation. I do. Confrontation is what separates the protagonist from the antagonist. If you think of a book, I bet you will always find some form of confrontation in there.

The important point is that the reader, one way or another, must reach the resolution and you are the only person who can take them there. You can make your story as complex or as simple as you wish, but it must have structure, it must have a pathway for the reader to take through the myriad twists and turns.

T – Rule of three AKA Triplets

The rule of three or triplets, is a similar concept to repetition. It involves emphasis and impact. It is a technique that allows the author to get the message home.

Here is one of my examples, from *The Stilling of the Heart:*

> 'The smell of <u>sweat and diesel and cheap perfume</u> mingled to create a nauseating clagginess that bit the back of the throat and raped the nostrils.'

What this does is present an image in the reader's mind. It attacks their senses. We all know the smell of sweat and diesel and how overwhelming cheap perfume can be. Smell relates to taste. They cannot exist without each other and because of life's experiences, the reader will not only smell these things, they will taste them, because they have had that experience before.

Listen to Ian Fleming at the beginning of *Casino Royale:*

> 'The <u>scent and smoke and sweat</u> of a casino are nauseating at three in the morning.'

This is how he opens the book. He takes the reader smack in there and assaults their senses. He doesn't present a pleasant picture, but he lets the reader know where they and the protagonist stand. Pretty much all of us will understand Fleming's words. We have (most of us) been stuck in smoke-filled rooms, stood next to a sweaty mongrel and we can search our senses' memories for what they recall of hot, crowded rooms and the myriad of smells that mug them at every turn.

It gives the reader a sense of time and place. It is yet another inclusive technique because it draws upon the reader's experience and through this, drags them in.

Once again, don't diminish the impact of the technique by overusing it. It's a great way to open a book, a chapter or a paragraph, because the reader is immediately asked to involve themselves in the sentence and encourages further reading. Used sparingly, it can elevate an ordinary paragraph into an involving, page turning piece of work.

One of my students, a cheeky and dangerous lass at the best of times, was having trouble distinguishing this from repetition.

I stood at the front of the class and said, 'Describe me in three words.'

Quick as a flash, she said, 'Old, fat and bald.'

She remembered the rule of three after that.

I certainly remembered her.

PART THREE:
POETRY

Poetry – What Is It?

1) Literature in metrical form; verse
2) The art or craft of writing verse
3) Anything resembling poetry in rhythm

Collins Concise Dictionary

I like this simple, down to earth definition:

The easiest way to recognize poetry is that it usually looks like poetry (remember what they say about ducks). While prose is organized with sentences and paragraphs, poetry is normally organized into lines.

www.creative-writing-now.com

This is a list of the types of poems.

Acrostic, Ballad, Ballade, Blank verse, Cinquain, Diamante, Echo Verse, Epic, Epigram, Free verse, Haiku, Horatian Ode, Irregular Ode, Kennings, Kyrielle, Limerick, Lyric, Ode, Ottava Rima, Pantoum, Pindaric Ode, Poem, Riddle, Rondeau, Senryu, Shape Poem, Shakespearean Sonnet, Sonnet, Tanka Poem, Terza Rima, Tetractys, Triolet, Tyburn

God above! Why? 33. 33 types of poem and I'm willing to bet that that's not all. I bet that in some dusty basement, at this moment, some light-blind, pale-skinned, nasal-voiced obsessive has come up with a new type of structure and name.

Seriously. I see a list like that and I just want to shoot myself. How does any of that help someone, especially schoolchildren, write a poem? How does it encourage anybody to write a poem? It doesn't. It's just that old snobby, pigeonholing, exclusivity thing cropping up again.

Everyone should just go by the www.creative-writing-now.com definition: 'it usually looks like poetry…is normally organized into lines'.

It's so much easier.

Just write!

Poetry is probably the most personal thing that you will write. It's very difficult to find distance in poetry because poetry tends to deal with emotions or make heartfelt statements. It is in its nature philosophical, confrontational, emotive. Poetry is often created from the need to escape the logical, as well as expressing feelings and other expressions in a tight, condensed manner.

Because of the differences between poetry and prose – the narrative, the more logical pathway in prose, the freer flow, a lack of need to keep to obvious metre, the less obvious structure – poetry has developed its own set of rules and regulations which, though often tedious, can also be used to the writer's advantage.

As I have said, there is a great deal of snobbery in poetry, more so than in prose. This could be because it is so much more specialised, so much more internalised and maybe more intellectualised. I don't like that kind of exclusivity. I think poetry is a wonderful form of self-expression and that people should not be intimidated by the 'poetry club set'. It brings about self-awareness and requires the writer to dig into those moist, dark places that other forms of writing do not. Everyone has a right to that. I'm certain that if more people wrote poetry, the world would be a much better place.

Saying this, I do believe that poetry needs to be defined and distinct from other styles of writing. It does need to have a set of boundaries that set it apart. This is not only for the writer, so that they can make the most of the poem's structure, but also because the reader needs to be able to come to grips with it and analyse it. People who read poetry don't mind analysing it, but they don't want it to be impenetrable. That merely renders it useless. It is the Sudoku of the written world. It must have mystery, but it must also have accessibility.

Poetry Meter

Meter is a way of measuring a line of poetry based on the rhythm of the words.

De-dum-de-dum-de-dum.

As a writer, being aware of meter helps you see clearly defined boundaries; it helps give structure to your work and increases your own word knowledge – you have to be able to adapt your vocabulary to the form of verse.

If you want to write poetry, knowing about meter will make you a better poet. It will help you understand what poets have done in the past, so that you can learn from them. It allows you to use traditional forms. Even if you prefer to write in free verse, you should learn about traditional forms. Being aware of traditions gives you more flexibility to use aspects of them when you want to or to 'break the rules' in a more interesting way.

Don't be confined by tradition. Build upon it.

THE MOIST PEARS

T - Tone
H - Hyperbole
E - Emotive Words

M - Metaphor
O - Onomatopoeia
I - Imagery
S - Simile
T - Theme

P - Personification
E - Enjambment
A - Alliteration
R - Rhyme / Repetition
S - Structure

Is this the worst mnemonic ever? Hell, yes. Is it one you'll ever forget? I doubt it.

T - Tone

Tone is the emotion within the poem. It lets the reader know the emotions of the subject of the poem or even the writer themselves. It can be sad, happy, mad, calm or angry. Anything.

Here is an example. It's a bit sweary but, hey ho:

'Look at you!
Just fucking look at you!
You're already dead!
I can see the resignation

Floating through
Your fucking head,
Like a putrid body
Rolling by,
Dead-eyed,
On the riverbed.'

This is from *Look at You* by me. It takes about ten seconds to recognise the tone. (Incidentally, Word wanted to change 'Your' to 'You're' – 6th line. I politely declined. Don't be fooled).

Now look at this:

What do I recall?
I recall barely anything at all.

A pond that shed its skin
As each new season sauntered in.
Sometimes, with a misty sigh,
Night chilled water
Fought with dawn's warm eye,
Shrouded fishermen and passers-by
And whispered of the changes soon to come
With the endless revolution of the sun.

From *Recall* - Chris Bradbury

The tone is altogether gentler, a little wistful; it walks instead of runs, whispers instead of rages. The reader will be less tense, will read it more slowly.

The words that I use to set the tone sends out a message to the reader, which is automatically picked up on. If they read this immediately after *Look at You*, it would be a relief. If they read them the other way around, it would be like diving into cold water after a soothing sauna.

That however, for me, is the point of poetry. It makes people think, lends comfort and discomfort. Even the kindest words can rage. Even the harshest words can be sighed. Poetry is great for delivering the unexpected.

H – Hyperbole

Hyperbole is gross exaggeration. I suppose all exaggeration is, by definition, gross, but if you take that exaggeration and big it up, that's hyperbole.

I would like to use Carol Anne Duffy and *Medusa* again, if I may. Her use of hyperbole in the poem is bitingly effective and creates imagery that, without the hyperbole, might not have been given a chance to shine.

> 'I stared in the mirror.
> Love gone bad
> Showed me a Gorgon.
> I stared at a dragon.'

Now, there is far more to this than simply hyperbole, but combining hyperbole with metaphor strikes a very powerful image. Of course, there was no gorgon there, but now that Ms Duffy has said that, that is what the reader sees. Why a dragon? It doesn't matter. What she sees in that mirror is a monster, not herself. Most of us see the crow's feet and the bags under our eyes and mutter a disconsolate, 'Shit!'. This poor woman sees no residue of herself, just the beast that she feels she has become. In her own eyes, she is beyond redemption.

In the next example, everything is bigger, in your face, so that you, the reader, will be submerged by the image that the writer wishes to present. Choice of words is vital if the writer is to get his message across.

> Largely unaware
> Of her heart giving in;
> Largely unaware
> Of her own propensity for sin,
> The sickly unsweet wedges herself
> Into place like so much rotten meat.
> She sticks out an arm, a trunk,
> Towards a brown paper bag,
> Snatches at it like a hungry dog,
> Shoves her face in deep,
> Sucks the cream
> From an innocent cake.

From *Hormones* - Chris Bradbury

The reader is supposed to be repulsed by the image. How does the writer do that? Look at the underlined words and try to replace them with something less impactful, something smaller. Omit those words, the concept dies.

Why does she 'suck' the cream from an 'innocent' cake? It represents on one level basic greed, a lack of self-control. We all find that repulsive in ourselves; no one likes to admit to a lack of self-control. On another level, she is 'sucking the life' out of an 'innocent'. It could be interpreted that she is sucking the life from those around her, her family and friends, without a thought for the consequences. On the first level, she gets fat and does a Mr Creosote[8]. On the other level, her selfish behaviour is slowly killing off her relationships, at home and outside of

---

[8] If you don't get this reference, go to Google and find it. Stop reading and watch Monty Python's Mr Creosote.

the home. She is using people to meet her own ends.

A final example is a very simple one from *Cherry Tree*, again, one of mine.

> …Forty-niner blackbirds
> Who proclaim their stake at break of day,
> Conceded by noon to casual passers-by,
> <u>Opportunistic magpies,</u>
> <u>The size of cats,</u>
> <u>Grown fat</u>
> <u>Upon spring lamb</u>.

Magpies are not the size of cats. If they were, I would not go out. That would be scary. Neither do they carry away lambs. That would be a challenge. What I'm saying is that, in the way of all magpies, they nick the newborn birds from the nest. It is a mix of hyperbole and metaphor to give the reader an idea of my perception of magpies.

If you cut or alter those words, the image that the writer wanted to get across fades, not just to a less effective image, but to nothing. Nobody wants nothing from a poem.

E - Emotive Words

Ah, the downfall of us all. Emotions. They are embarrassing, awkward, discomforting, nauseating. They involve such things as 'love' and 'hate', 'brave' and cruel'. They make the British sphincter rattle. They require the opening of sluice gates inside us that are normally left to leak and trickle harmlessly into the greater sea of life.

Yet we all like a good film, whether it be a weepie or an action-filled blockbuster. We all like our TV series such as Game of Thrones or Downton Abbey. We all (I'm assuming this of you, if you are reading this) like to be swept away of the current of emotions in a book. My wife, who doesn't cry or she will dehydrate and need to be drip-fed, has cried at Stephen King's *The Green Mile*, like a baby and at the first part of *Harry Potter and the Deathly Hallows*. She says that she 'cried buckets' at that. I thought the reservoirs were low that day.

I cried at the end of *Cujo* and *On Her Majesty's Secret Service*, I admit. Music constantly brings a lump to my throat.

So emotions and emotive words are an essential part of our art. This can be applied to poetry, prose and even articles.

As previously mentioned, Seamus Heaney's *Follower*, is a giant piece of work. He takes us on a trip across generations, almost anecdotally then, at the end, sticks the knife in.

> 'I was a nuisance, tripping, falling,
> Yapping always. But today
> It is my father who keeps stumbling
> Behind me, and will not go away.'

He is not overtly emotional through the poem, but he gradually builds the tale and gets the reader's empathy through nostalgia, through the father/son relationship, which hits those who had it and those who didn't equally as hard, then he snatches it away. It is almost cruel in its execution, but it remains a favourite of mine because of how he did it. Anybody else would have cocked it up.

This, on the other hand, drives me potty:

And on that cheek, and o'er that brow,

So soft, so calm, yet eloquent,
The smiles that win, the tints that glow,
But tell of days in goodness spent,
A mind at peace with all below,
A heart whose love is innocent!

From *She Walks in Beauty* – Lord Byron

It is a great poem; there is no doubt about it. It has all the dum-de-dum-de-dum that you want and all those lovely 'o'ers', but it has no grit.

This is just my opinion and I accept that I am wrong. It's already making me react, so it must be doing something right.

My wife says that poetry that doesn't rhyme and have dum-de-dum-de-dum, just isn't poetry. She's right too. Why? Because that's what she likes and art caters for all tastes.

I'll leave this part with some of the best emotive poetry I know. It has perfect balance. You might recognise it. It was used to superb effect by John Hannah in the film *Four Weddings and a Funeral*. I would recommend you watch it. Also, see if you can find Richard Burton's *Addlestrop* and *Do Not Go Gentle Into That Good Night* by Dylan Thomas. Listening to a professional read these works gives a completely new insight into them.

Twelve Songs - IX - WH Auden (Stanzas 1 & 4)

Stop all the clocks, cut off the telephone,
Prevent the dog from barking with a juicy bone,
Silence the pianos and with muffled drum
Bring out the coffin, let the mourners come.

The stars are not wanted now: put out every one;
Pack up the moon and dismantle the sun;
Pour away the ocean and sweep up the wood;
For nothing now can ever come to any good.

Why does this work? It works because it raises empathy in the reader. Those who have lost someone precious will understand the need to stop the world, to dispense with all frivolity. There is nothing left that is beautiful in this world, so get rid of it all. Even those who have not lost will be left in no doubt about the devastation wrought by this death.

M – Metaphor

What is the difference between a metaphor and a simile? This is often a stumbling block for many would-be writers.

I'm just going to define a metaphor for now and leave the simile to the simile section, but it is something that we should all know. It is important for all types of creative writing.

A metaphor compares two unlike objects to put an image in the reader's head.

For example:

Pig face. (Come on, we've all used it)
He has the legs of a donkey. (The recent England team in the Euros)

Medusa, that poem that I keep harping on about (justifiably I say), is essentially one long metaphor. The woman has become a monster. No, she hasn't, not literally. Here are the opening lines:

'A suspicion, a doubt, a jealousy
Grew in my mind,
<u>Which turned the hairs on my head to filthy
snakes</u>'

Her hair did not become filthy snakes. She might well have neglected herself for a while and her hair might need a damn good wash, but there were no snakes. She is merely making a comparison between two unlike things, herself and a monster, in order to present an image to the reader.

You will see the difference between this and a simile shortly.

This is from *The Battle of Wakefield Road*, one of my poems.

<u>In the distance lies the holy citadel</u>,
Its gates shut tight since <u>blood-red sunset</u> fell

This was not about a holy citadel; it was about a bus depot that was involved in a strike. It became a place of safety, a place of defence, a Jerusalem for which to fight. It gave the reader a sense of objective laced with peril, a sense of sanctuary and, combined with the 'blood-red sunset', warned of things to come.

As a writing technique, I prefer the metaphor to the simile. It is subtler, more open to discussion and interpretation and makes the reader (and writer) work a little harder to extract meaning, thus getting greater reward from the work.

O – Onomatopoeia

Turning sound into words. The buzz of a bee, because a bee buzzes. The bang of a gun, because a gun bangs. It is that simple. The hiss of a snake. The whoosh of a wave. The word represents, in sound, the noise.

Here are a couple of lines form Edgar Allen Poe's *The Bells*:

> Silver bells !
> What a world of merriment their melody foretells !
> How they <u>tinkle, tinkle, tinkle</u>,
> In the icy air of night !

How easy is that?

I – Imagery

Imagery is putting a picture in the reader's mind. Quite often you will find a combination of techniques, for example enjambment, metaphor and onomatopoeia coming together to create an image.

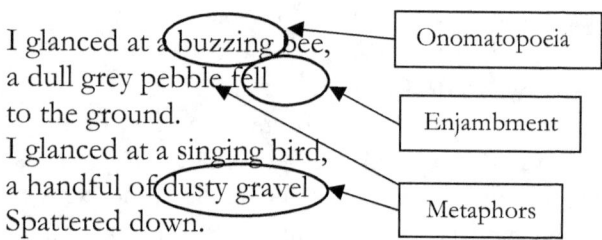

I glanced at a buzzing bee,
a dull grey pebble fell
to the ground.
I glanced at a singing bird,
a handful of dusty gravel
Spattered down.

Here, in Carol Ann Duffy's *Medusa*, we have three techniques coming together to reinforce the image of Medusa, she who turns living objects to stone with a single glance.

We will come to enjambment soon. It is simply the absence of punctuation at the end of a line of poetry.

Imagery could of course be quite simple, as in this extract from *The Stilling of the Heart*:

> 'Tassin looked out at the horizon. Before him, in <u>all its splendour</u>, was a <u>summer</u> <u>sunset</u>. It <u>lay across the sky in a kaleidoscope of colours</u> and <u>reflected</u> upon the still sea, as if the sea itself had been hypnotised by the end of days.'

Imagery does still combine with other techniques for a fuller effect, but it stands alone too and presents the reader with a picture that they have stored in their memory. The reader's own experiences bring so much to the written piece. It is up to the writer to revive those perhaps dormant experiences

S – Simile

What is a **simile**?

Understandably, people often get these and metaphors confused. They both involve comparison, but metaphors tend to be a little deeper and, sometimes, a little darker.

A safe rule to follow is that if it has the words 'like' or 'as' in it, it's a simile.

> 'That cat is as big as a dog'
> 'She was like a perfect rose.'
> 'That banana tasted like Heaven.'

T – Theme

What is your work about? Is it about jealousy or greed? Any one of the seven sins could be a theme. A piece of work can have more than one theme.

Think of *Gone with the Wind*. The themes are war, love, possession and slavery. The theme of *A Beginner's Guide to the Wars of the Roses* is, unsurprisingly, the Wars of the Roses.

What does tend to be the case with themes is that there is one main theme, which can have several sub-themes. In the case of *Gone with the Wind,* it would probably be in this order:

1) Love
2) War
3) Possession
4) Slavery

Three and four could be swapped around, possibly even integrated. It is important for the writer to have a clear theme so that the reader and the characters know where they stand.

It gets a little more difficult with abstract work such as Camus' *The Outsider* or *The Plague* because he will use allegory and metaphor to represent the abstract concept behind his work, but a theme will always be there.

If you think of any book you have read, you will find a theme and probably some sub-themes rumbling away underneath.

In poetry, the principles are the same. The difference is that the writer has less time to get that theme across and must therefore be more focussed.

If you take Tennyson's *The Charge of the Light Brigade*, the primary theme is war, but within the framework, you can find duty, courage and death. Beyond this, you could look at the jingoism and the propaganda value to the country.

When writing a poem, you will have a theme in mind. Quite naturally, you will find that, like a river, it springs tributaries that remain relevant to the main theme and yet have a life of their own.

Here are some stanzas that contain themes within the poem:

In the distance lies the holy citadel,   Cause
Its gates shut tight since blood-red sunset fell,
No natural sound disturbs the night's dark spell,
While in the soulless shadows, the unimagined dwells.   Fear

There are different truths that hide in night and day,   Politics
Each quicksand built and prone to quick decay.
Each man must choose which truth to use today   Confrontation
And sleepless take his sword into the fray.

'Are you happy now?' decry the Dervish screams,
As inch by inch I run the thrashing stream.
'I hope that cancer steals your children's dreams!'
Cry men who once broke bread and rode   Loyalty/Betrayal

with me.

Don't lose focus upon the main theme, but use those other themes to reinforce atmosphere, reason, to present the bigger picture and increase the reader's understanding of the main theme.

In such a short, tight space, the impact of every word is vital. Don't use words that you don't need and make sure you choose the right word to deliver the strongest punch. You will find that no poet will ever waste a word. Every word, every piece of punctuation, is there for a reason.

P – Personification

This is where the writer gives a non-human, human characteristics.

In my poem *Her Dog Was Fat,* I write these lines about a dog:

> 'Except to its bowl where it sucked water
> Like a toothless old man.'

The reader immediately has something to compare it to, something to relate to, because I have given the dog human characteristics.

Wordsworth's *I Wandered Lonely as a Cloud* presents the personification of nature to great effect:

> 'When all at once <u>I saw a crowd</u>,
> A <u>host</u>, of golden daffodils;
> Beside the lake, beneath the trees,
> Fluttering and <u>dancing</u> in the breeze.
>
> …Ten thousand saw I at a glance,

Tossing their heads in sprightly <u>dance</u>.'

E – Enjambment

Enjambment is a weapon well used. What does it do? It allows the poem to flow, it makes metaphors and similes stand out, it helps the poem keep its rhythm. It guides the reader with that Enigma code that is punctuation.

I want to show you now what enjambment can do and to do that I'm returning to Carol Ann Duffy and *Medusa:*

> 'And here you come
> with a shield for a heart
> and a sword for a tongue
> and your girls, your girls.
> Wasn't I beautiful?
> Wasn't I fragrant and young?'

What Ms Duffy does is combine techniques to masterful (mistressful?) effect. In this one stanza lie metaphors, direct address, repetition and rhetorical questions.

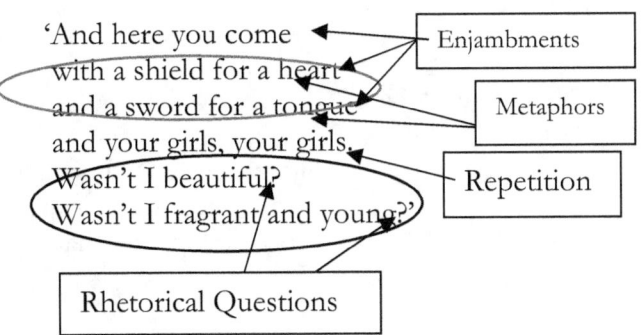

It's an outstanding stanza.

The enjambments do two things. They allow the reader to read without pausing for punctuation, but they also make the following metaphors stand out. It is the very absence of punctuation that allows the poem to breathe and the other techniques to come alive. Direct address leads to enjambment, which leads to metaphor, which leads to enjambment, which is followed by a metaphor and an enjambment. It then leads into the next line, which has the punctuation *in the middle* of it in the form of a comma, which means that the reader is forced to pause and take note of the repetition. You can hear the tiredness and despair in the poor woman's voice as she repeats 'your girls, your girls'. Then it goes bang into the rhetorical questions. These plead for recognition, for hope, for affirmation.

None of this is accidental. They are there to let you feel the emotions of the character, to let you understand the intentions of the writer and to allow you, the reader, to be able to read the poem to its full effect and to *feel* it. It is a set of coded instructions to the reader about how to interpret and read these lines.

And you know what? My wife would hate this poem because it's free form and doesn't rhyme.

A - Alliteration

We have covered alliteration quite thoroughly in the section on Prose. However, it never hurts to put a bit of context to it and see it in a poem. I'm sure that you will know this one:

'What is this life if, full of care,
We have no time to <u>stand and stare</u>.
No time to stand <u>beneath the boughs</u>
And stare as long as sheep or cows.
No time to see, <u>when woods we</u> pass,
Where squirrels hide their nuts in grass.
No time to see, in broad daylight,
<u>Streams</u> full of <u>stars, like skies</u> at night'.

From *Leisure* - William Henry Davies

Even though the alliteration-involved words are occasionally not next to each other, the effect is still there.

Don't underestimate alliteration's benefits to the reader. Neither should you underestimate the use of this technique in lending rhythm to your work and in making it more readable.

R - Rhyme
Repetition

Rhyme is a multi-purpose tool. It grabs the reader's attentions to make something memorable, it looks appealing when each line is tidy (pleasing structure draws the reader in) and it is pleasing to the ear.

Rhyme can be obvious:

'What's that fluttering in the <u>breeze</u>?
It's just a piece of cloth
That brings a nation to its <u>knees</u>.'

From *Flag* - John Agard

Four out of five stanzas maintain this pattern, then

the fifth changes it slightly:

> 'How can I possess such a cloth?
> Just ask for a flag my <u>friend</u>.
> Then blind your conscience to the <u>end</u>.'

It goes against expectations. The reader has become comfortable with the rhythm and rhyme and might by now have become immune to the underlying message of the poem.

But with the change in rhyme comes a change in tone and because the reader has to do a bit more work to maintain the rhyme and the rhythm, the words stand out more and the darkness behind them leaps to the fore.

In *Harmonium* by Simon Armitage, there is still rhyme, but the reader has to work that little bit harder to find it and work with the punctuation to highlight it.

> 'But its hummed harmonics still struck a
> <u>chord</u>:
> for a hundred years that organ had stood
> by the choristers' <u>stalls</u>, where father and
> son,
> each in their time, had opened their <u>throats</u>
> and gilded finches – like high <u>notes</u> – had
> streamed out.'

The punctuation forces the reader to notice the rhyme. Once the reader has noticed this, it is a lot easier to read and the meaning in the poem is much more easily found.

Armitage never makes it easy. It's almost as if the confrontation within his work is aimed at the reader too, in order to make them work for their reward. It's usually worth it.

Don't forget though, that rhyme does not stand alone. In *Flag*, it is combined with enjambment and a rhetorical question. In *Harmonium*, it combines with enjambment and it is vital that Armitage gets the punctuation spot on, so that the reader can extract the maximum from the work in the way that Armitage wants them to.

In one of my poems, *Condition of Life*, I wanted to take a different approach to the rhyme. I wrote it as a block of text and, to make it a little easier for the reader, highlighted the rhyming areas.

'The cat **cracked** its **back**, slimed along the **ground**, dead eyes fixed, no breaths, no **sound**, belly drenched in early **dew**, fat paws spread, clown's **shoes,** tail **trailed** through a dark green **wake**, a lifeless **slug**, through October **fug**, the miasma of night and **day**, the cloud of senses; dead **leaves**, fresh **breeze**, mulch and mushroom, spored wood in slow **decay**, false shadows, false **gold**, the stain of earth grown **old**, all set **aside** with each stuttered **stride**, a desert-lizard-**dance**, gene-led-**trance**, one step at a **time**, each patient, measured, balanced **pace**, a statement of **intent**, a silent slo-mo **chase,** accepted stalking of **innocence**, no intention of **malevolence**, merely instinct, to **be**, no sorrow, no regret, no reason, no **integrity** and on such a **tide,** on such **purity**, such freedom, the bird, in virtue, **died**.'

Should I have highlighted those words? In hindsight, it might have been a bit patronising to have done so and is does show a bit too much of a need in me to be understood. Neither of those occurred to me when I did it. I just liked the look of it and the idea of it, but was I *really* thinking of the reader at the time? Possibly not.

Repetition has already been approached in the Prose section; however, because of the nature of poetry - the confined space, the need to maintain meter, etc - its effects are immediately more noticeable and potentially more devastating. In prose, the repetition if often surrounded by exposition, so it is a small part of a many-pronged attack.

In poetry, is there as a primary weapon in the onslaught upon the reader's senses.

If we go back to *Flag*, there is one line that is repeated for four of the five stanzas:

'It's just a piece of cloth'.

Why? Why did John Agard, in each of his three line stanzas, use this as the middle line?

Partly because it highlights the devastating changes in stanza five, lulls the reader into a false sense of security.

There is perhaps a sense of irony, because he knows and we know what the flag represents - the worst of colonialism, of empire, of borders, of war, of conquest. The flag goes from being an inconsequential piece of cloth to being a symbol of dead conscience and oppression.

Going back to *Harmonium*, Simon Armitage uses only one piece of repetition in the poem:

And one of its notes had lost its tongue,

and holes were worn in both the treadles
where the organist's feet, in grey, woollen
socks
and leather-soled shoes, had <u>pedalled and
pedalled.</u>

Why has he saved this technique for this one place
in the entire poem? It is to show the miles done. As Indiana
Jones says in *Raiders of the Lost Ark:* 'It's not the age, honey;
it's the mileage'.

He is describing an old instrument that is gathering
dust in a church. It speaks of the relentless assault upon
the harmonium over the years. One 'pedalled' would have
merely stated what an organist *did* with his leather-soled
shoes; the repetition speaks, subtly, of the *effect* of what he
did.

S – Structure

Ah, the *capo di tutti capi.* The boss of all bosses. In
poetry, structure is vital. There is a saying that we eat our
meals twice: once with our eyes and once with our bellies.
It is the same with written work.

If you don't like the look of something, you aren't
going to eat it.

We have already seen in the Prose section how the
look of a page dictates how the reader approaches that
page or even if they approach it at all.

You have also seen the 'List of 33'.

Each one of those 33 has a different structure.

So of what is structure in poetry comprised?

Stanzas, punctuation, syllables, single lines,
rhyming couplets.

Even the number of lines per stanza gives that type

of stanza a name.

couplet (2 lines)
tercet (3 lines)
quatrain (4 lines)
cinquain (5 lines)
sestet (6 lines)
septet (7 lines)
octave (8 lines)

Then there is Iambic pentameter, Trochaic pentameter, Anapaestic pentameter and Dactylic pentameter. Don't be afraid, it's just a way of measuring syllables and rhythm. You will find these on your own, by accident, without even worrying about them. Once you begin putting words down, your curiosity will get the better of you and you will quite naturally develop an interest in these things.

I don't know what '-ameter' most of my poems are in. I thump out the syllables with my fingers and if it sounds or feels right, it's away.

Poems could carry the form of:

A Ballad
An Elegy
An Epic
A Lyric
A Narrative
A Sonnet

How many types of sonnet are there? Oh, let me count the ways!

There is also a difference between **form** and

structure. I shall leave it to a wiser person than I to differentiate between the two[9].

> **'Form** relates to the external shape of a text, determined by how it is presented on paper, organised by stanzas/paragraphs, lines, syllables, rhyme, justification – best thought of as a silhouette.
>
> **Structure** is more interesting because it goes beyond the visible...displaying the organic relationship between ideas, feelings and attitudes within a text.
> For example, the form of a sonnet is its 14 line length...Within that form the structure may be 8 lines of description leading to 6 lines of reflection, generalisation, resolution; or the mood may go from neutral to sombre, or from sombre and resentful to acceptant.'

At this stage, none of this matters.

Just write.

I don't care about your spelling, your structure or your form. I am a zombie writer. I want your brains.

There is an important point to be made here though, about all of this. There is not just madness behind the 33 names, the form and the structure and the punctuation; there is reason.

The reason is that you, as a writer, want to be understood and you want your readers to understand you. You have a burning, unquenched desire to communicate.

---

[9] www.mrswilliamsgcseenglish.blogspot.co.uk

It is completely selfish, genetic even, but if you don't do it...God help those around you.

All these elements in THE MOIST PEARS will help you, but each one must be weighed carefully before being added to your poem's recipe. Too much of one ingredient can ruin a fine meal.

PART FOUR:
PLAYS/SCREENPLAYS

What Is A Play?

'A dramatic composition written for actors for performance on a stage'

Collins Concise Dictionary

Them with high-falutin', rootin'-tootin' speech say:

'The first act is the Protasis, or exposition.
The second act is the Epitasis, or complication.
The final act is the Catastrophe, or resolution.'[10]

'The difference between fiction and drama is simply that in a play the story has to be told almost exclusively in dialogue.'

Writing for pleasure and Profit - Michael Legat

I say: 'Give it a beginning, a middle and an end'.

Dialogue

It doesn't matter if you're Shakespeare, Harold Pinter, Charles Dickens or Quentin Tarantino, the words in dialogue matter.

The dialogue should tell you all you need to know. You should be able to pick up anxiety, happiness, fear,

---

[10] www.playwriting101.com

tiredness, hate or any other emotion in the words. This is why Elmore Leonard said that no more than 'said... needs to be said'. Let your words talk for you, but more importantly, let them talk for your character.

Let's compare two writers, Elmore Leonard and Quentin Tarantino:

The first part is from the end of the restaurant scene in *Reservoir Dogs* by Quentin Tarantino.

The second part is from *Rum Punch* by Elmore Leonard.

Reservoir Dogs by Quentin Tarantino

NICE GUY EDDIE
Okay, everybody cough up green for the little lady.
Everybody whips out a buck, and throws it on the table. Everybody, that is, except Mr Pink.
C'mon, throw in a buck.

MR PINK
Uh-uh. I don't tip.

NICE GUY EDDIE
Whaddaya mean, you don't tip?

MR PINK
I don't believe in it.

NICE GUY EDDIE
You don't believe in tipping?

MR BROWN

(laughing)
I love this guy, he's a madman, this guy.

MR BLONDE
Do you have any idea what these ladies make? They make shit.

MR PINK
Don't give me that. She don't make enough money, she can quit.
Everybody laughs.

NICE GUY EDDIE
I don't even know a Jew who'd have the balls to say that. So let's get this straight. You never ever tip?

MR PINK
I don't tip because society says I gotta. I tip when somebody deserves a tip. When somebody really puts forth an effort, they deserve a little something extra. But this tipping automatically, that shit's for the birds. As far as I'm concerned, they're just doin' their job.

MR BLUE
Our girl was nice.

MR PINK
Our girl was okay. She didn't do anything special.

Rum Punch by Elmore Leonard.

'I said, "Renee, I'm working. I'm trying to save a young man from doing ten years and I'm waiting for him to call." I try to explain it to her in a nice way. You know what she said? She said, "Well, I'm working too."'

Winston seemed to smile. It was hard to tell. He said, 'I was out there one time. Renee acted like she didn't see me and I'm the only person in there.'

'That's what I mean,' Max said. 'She says she's working -doing what? You never see anybody unless she's got the wine and cheese out. You know what I mean? For a show. Then you have all the freeloaders. You see these guys, they look like they live in cardboard boxes under the freeway, they're eating everything, drinking the wine . . . You know who they are? The artists and their crowd. I've even recognized guys I've written. Renee's playing like she's Peter Pan, has her hair cut real short, and all these assholes are the Lost Boys. The place clears out, she hasn't sold one fucking painting.'

'So what you're telling me,' Winston said, 'you're still supporting her habit.'

'She's got a Cuban guy now, David, I mean Da-veed, she says is gonna be discovered and make it big, any day now. The guy's a busboy at Chuck and Harold's.'

What you might see is that, although one piece is

written for a book and the other a screenplay, what drives the characters (and pushes the reader on) is the dialogue.

What do we learn? We learn in *Reservoir Dogs* that Mr Pink is a tight-wad. We learn that Nice Guy Eddie is anti-Semitic. We learn that Mr Blonde and Nice Guy Eddie have a social conscience. This lets the audience know that these guys, these vicious criminals, have a decent side. It lends empathy. We know that Mr Pink is a man of principle who doesn't like to be emotionally manipulated, who is pragmatic, regardless of the cost to others.

What about *Rum Punch?* Max is a snob and possibly slightly racist, sarcastic and his relationship has failed, leaving him angry. We learn that Renée is a stuck pin in the butt.

All these things come from a few lines of dialogue.

There are 'stage directions', as in a stage-play, in the screenplay, and only the barest extraneous material (unlike most prose) in Leonard's book. Both writers allow their characters (and readers) to breathe, with a careful eye on the reader being able to keep pace with what's been written.

Stage plays and films rely upon the visual aspect, that is why we go to 'see' a play or a movie.

Leave the action/stage directions to the director. If you need to move the actors or get them to react in a certain way to further the plot, then do so; if you don't, let the director decide. Once again though, what you want from the actors should be conveyed in the dialogue.

It's no different to what Shakespeare was doing four hundred years ago:

King Lear - Act 3 Scene 2

Another part of the heath. Storm still.

Enter KING LEAR and Fool

KING LEAR
Blow, winds, and crack your cheeks! rage!
blow!
You cataracts and hurricanoes, spout
Till you have drench'd our steeples,
drown'd the cocks!
You sulphurous and thought-executing
fires,
Vaunt-couriers to oak-cleaving
thunderbolts,
Singe my white head! And thou, all-
shaking thunder,
Smite flat the thick rotundity o' the world!
Crack nature's moulds, an germens spill at
once,
That make ingrateful man!

The above passage is relentlessly emotional, both in the dialogue and in the setting. An old man, a discarded king, is out on the heath, in the foulest of weather and is now tipping over the precipice into madness, driven by guilt.

Yet we only see a couple of directions at the top.

The words need minimal stage direction, so we are presented at the beginning with a scene and the cast – no more. The actors interpret the lines though punctuation, what they know about the characters and the words.

In my own play *Uncomfortably Numb*, the same rules apply, despite the fact that it is a far more abstract piece, with a different theme and tone:

ACT 1

Bird and Burton sit behind a desk each. Their jackets are off and hang on the backs of their chairs. The sleeves of their white shirts are rolled up. Their ties hand loose around their necks. They are doing their best not to notice each other. An uneasy silence prevails.

Burton: (suddenly, jovially) Beautiful morning!

Bird: (tiredly) Is it?

Burton: (less enthusiastically) I thought so. Do you disagree? If you do, please say so.

Bird: I can't say. The morning has escaped me. Or perhaps I escaped the morning. Either way, I didn't see it. But I'll take your word for it, that it was good.

Burton: Thank you. (pauses to pluck up the courage to speak) Have you been here long?

Bird: Not so long. I've been here longer. You?

Burton: Not so long as you. Long enough though. I could have been elsewhere you know. I was invited elsewhere, but I didn't go.

Bird: (interested) Where could you have gone?

Burton: Anywhere. I could have gone anywhere. I don't have to be here. If I wanted, I could leave. Just like that. (fails to click his fingers) Couldn't you?

Bird: I suppose so, if I felt inclined.

I wrote this some years ago. I love it, but I should have left more to the actors. The words actually give enough direction in themselves.

What this was, was a young fella being a little too OCD for his own good. I could have skipped eighty percent of the bracketed material. The exposition at the top would have sufficed. Being there, the brackets do not make the work less effective, but it would certainly annoy the hell out of some actors and directors and act as an unnecessary distraction. Sorry chaps and chapesses.

With plays and screenplays, as with prose and poetry, you still require a narrative, you still need that pathway down which to lead your listener/viewer/reader. There is a slight change in the priority of composition, that's all. Dialogue becomes that much more important. Make it natural, make it real. Listen to others speak. Obviously, don't put all the 'ums' and 'ahs' in. If your character has a stutter, the actor will do that. If they are nervous, the actor with show that. That is why we have actors and directors, to bring your words to life.

If you are going to delve into this world, make sure that you research it. There are plenty of screenplays available on the net or to buy in book form. A favourite of mine is *Withnail and I* by Bruce Robinson. It has to be one of the great writer/director/actor collaborations because, although Robinson's script is superb, as director he enabled the actors to bring what he had written to life. It is a perfectly cast, acted and directed piece of work and a lesson for all of us. And the end still moves me to the verge of tears each time

PART FIVE:
ARTICLES

Articles crop up everywhere; in newspapers, magazines, on billboards, placards, on the web, in professional magazines, even on leaflets - a leaflet *is* a small article. They, at first glance, seem throwaway. That's good. It is the ease on the eye that matters, the clever psychology behind the headlines and the paragraphs and the images.

If you look at a newspaper or magazine, you will see articles by the dozen and each one of them will be laid out exactly as the editor wanted it to be. Nothing is there by accident.

FISHCLUBB

Competing for the worst mnemonic ever is FISHCLUBB.

FISHCLUBB.

How on earth did this come about? Was it invented by a violent fisherman? Was it an exclusive club for fish, hidden among the seaweed and the coral, where they read small books and played chess? Or was it the only mnemonic that someone could come up with that contained those letters?

I'll go with number three.

I have never forgotten it though.

F - Fonts
I - Images
S - Slogans
H - Headings
C - Colours
L - Layout
U - Underline
B - Bold text
B - Bullets

If you look at the next page, you'll see an article from the Barnsley Chronicle.

See how much of FISHCLUBB is used. There is a lot of thought goes into every article in every magazine and newspaper.

Once you've had a peek, we'll go through them.

Font

Colours

Headings

Bold

Love is in the air for visitors to the Civic

BY GAIL ROBINSON

IT'S all about the LOVE at the Civic this month.

An Olivier Award nominee, one night gigs in sleazy northern clubs, randy Gods, psychotic giants and murderous elves, and a feisty 70-year-old – love conquers all at the Civic.

● Caroline Horton is bringing her highly acclaimed one-woman show Penelope Retold, revisiting the adaptation of the Odyssey from the point of view of Odysseus' wife.

This is a theatrical storm that sweeps through poetry, songs, comedy and YouTube clips towards a poignant and furious conclusion.

Olivier award nominee and Stage best solo performer, Caroline, presents an epic tale of love, loneliness and the need to be free.

Penelope Retold is on April 16.

● Set against a world of gigs in sleazy northern clubs, Roberts and John Productions present Satin 'n' Steel.

A karaoke competition brings together seasoned pro, Vince Steel, and talented beginner, Teena White, in an explosion of talent and creativity. He persuades her to form a duo – and to change her name.

As the all-singing and all-dancing Satin 'n' Steel, they set their sights on the big time. And as love blossoms, it seems nothing could go wrong, but a secret threatens to jeopardise their plans.

Satin 'n' Steel is on April 18.

● After touring Unmithable around the world, the award-winning company Temple Theatre take audiences on a riotous journey through the world of the Vikings with new show Norsesome.

Audiences will witness the adventures of Thor, Loki, Odin and many others, in a show that combines comedy, drama and songs.

Norsesome is on April 23.

● Finally, Vamos Theatre, the UK's leading full mask theatre company, is bringing its latest national touring production to Barnsley.

Nursing Lives is a love story set in the early 1980s of Thatcher's Britain and the hard-working, heartbreaking, swing-dancing world of the UK's wartime hospitals.

When Flo, a feisty 70-something, learns that the hospital she trained at during the Second World War is being demolished, she decides to take one last look – and stop the bulldozers in their tracks.

Nursing Lives is at the Civic on April 11. Visit barnsleycivic.co.uk or call 327000.

SONG AND DANCE: **Satin 'n' Steel is on April 18.**

VIKINGS: **Norsesome is performed on April 23.**

Layout

Bullets

Bold

Images

F - Fonts

I was working once with some students on a comparison of three websites. Part of the comparison involved layout, which led to fonts.

Two out of the three were fine, but every student (and the tutor) said that the third one was 'horrible'. It was a universal dislike.

When we took a closer look, a large part of their dislike was because the site used far too many font sizes. It was all over the place. This meant that the 'silhouette' of the piece, that important first glance, was unimpressive. On closer examination, it made the piece look untidy and unprofessional and finally, they had to work too hard to get to the nitty gritty. The site was asking them to strain their eyes, constantly readjust their vision, to pick out the important bits.

This applies to any kind of writing. Do not make the reader uncomfortable. They should be able to keep an equal distance throughout the piece without having to move the page back and forth or squint to see what it says. On computer screens you could almost double that rule because the eye strain caused by staring at a bright screen is considerable anyway, but to have to constantly change focus can lead to a feeling of sea-sickness, especially if there is some heavy scrolling to do.

The article above does fonts perfectly. It uses the same font, for a start, which is more aesthetically pleasing than jumping about all over with different font types. The font size is gradually reduced as you work your way past the headline. Once past that and the small sub-headline, there is a consistent font size. This makes for much easier and more comfortable reading. There is a fair chance that, if the content is good enough, the reader will reach the end of the piece.

I - Images

Images litter our pages and our web sites, our glossy magazines and even our graphic novels.

Why?

Well, they reinforce the text for a start. A picture really does say a thousand words. If you look at, for example, Amazon's web site, there is not one picture there that serves no purpose. You can click on any image and it will take you to the relevant text or half a dozen other pictures.

It is a selling site that sticks resolutely to its cause, but in a very appealing manner - it's like walking through your own private mall, but without the smells of the public, fast food and random banjo players.

It is the same for an article in a newspaper or on a blog. That picture will give the reader an image, which will reinforce the text next to it. The two pictures show you the acts involved in the article. They are shown so that the reader has something, some*body*, to which they can relate. This can also help sell tickets and, with a little wording beneath, neatly paraphrase the article.

S - Slogans

- Every Little Helps.
- I'm Lovin' It. (not in my case!)
- Your Flexible Friend
- Vorsprung Durch Technik

I bet you know all of those slogans.

I have one - 'Just Write...'

Nobody knows that one...yet.

Every successful major advertising campaign has a great slogan.

In Bill Bryson's made In America, he talks about the Ford Edsel, one of the biggest failures in American car manufacture, famously so.

'In 1952 Ford began work on a secret project it called the *E car*.

Huge care was taken with choosing a name. Ford's advertising agency, Foote, Cone and Belding, drew up a list of 18,000 suggestions, and Ford staff added a further 2,500. The poet Marianne Moore was commissioned to come up with a list of names, and offered such memorable, if unusable suggestions as the *Mongoose Civique*, the *Utopian Turtletop*, the *Pluma Piluma*, the *Pastelogram*, the *Resilient Bullet*, the *Varsity Stroke* and the *Andante con Moto*.

All of these were carefully whittled down to a short-list of sixteen names. On 8 November 1956 an executive committee met to make the final choice. After much discussion it reduced the list to four favoured names: *Corsair, Citation, Ranger* and

Pacer. Then, for reasons that are much disputed (largely because no one wished afterwards to be actively associated with the choice) the panel members opted for a name not on the list: *Edsel.*

It was named for Edsel Ford, Henry and Clara Ford's only child…'

One slogan was:

'The thrill starts with the grille.' (see picture below[11])

It just shows that sometimes, no matter what you do, you will not win. And it's a great story.

Where did it fail? Henry Ford rejected 20,500 suggestions, expert suggestions, to use the name of his son. Sometimes it's worth listening to advice.

Oh, that and the car was very badly made.

The thrill starts with the grille

(And never seems to end)

> Cultural critics speculated that the car was a flop because the vertical grill looked like a vagina. Maybe. America in the '50s was certainly phobic about the female business.
>
> *www.content.time.com*

---

[11] From https://fi.pinterest.com/pin/52213676899967834/

You must pick your slogan very carefully and combine it with all the other factors - the visuals, the voices, the music, the font, your target market – and then you might get some way towards achieving your goal.

Don't forget your target market. Everything has a target market. This book has a target market. I had to think about that before I wrote the first word. It would be no good going into the muddy, bloody depths of English grammar and construction, deconstructing the heart of literature, if all I really want you to do is have some fun writing. Which is exactly what I want.

For a writer of prose, there is ample opportunity for slogans - the title of the book, chapter titles, a recurring phrase. It's the same with any form of writing.

H - Headings

The article has a headline and a sub-headline. The headline is there for two reasons:

11) To attract your attention
12) To summarise what is being said underneath

(just going back a few chapters, I am apparently writing in American today)

'LOVE IS IN THE AIR FOR VISITORS TO THE CIVIC'

If we break it down a bit, what are the significant words? Love. Visitors. Civic. Probably those three. If the headline were just those three words, we would probably get the gist of it.

Anyone who is interested in love and the Civic, the local theatre, will probably read on.

Beneath that is a sub-headline, which expounds

upon this statement.

'It's all about LOVE at the Civic this month'

'Love is in capitals, so this reinforces what they wanted you to see in the headline. The Civic gets another mention - reinforcement.

No words are wasted and important points are hammered home, but in a way that will appeal, rather than repulse.

Make your headline mean something. Use alliteration

'SEXY CIVIC SELLS LOVE'

or other writing techniques. The same applies to leaflets or posters. Use colours, capitals, bold, underlining – whatever you want.

C - Colours

There are limitations, mainly expense, in publishing. For me, I had to make this book black and white. It was the same for *A Beginner's Guide to the Wars of the Roses*. Had I used colour, you would have been asked to pay too much. I don't want to drive people away, so I compromise and have black and white graphics. Word is very helpful with all this though.

Advertisers will talk about 'white space', that precious area between the pictures, which allows the eyes to rest and the images to stand out. It is the gaps between the notes.

They will use colour to attract you in the same way that flowers attract bees. It is a basic animal instinct turned into the psychology of selling.

In the newspaper article, the journalist's name is in colour. Why? Well, it makes her name stand out. If you like what she has written, you will search for more of her articles. The popularity of the articles might well mean more sales for the paper. So, in the long and short term, colour can be a good investment.

The colour photographs again draw you to the page. If you like what you see, you'll go for the honey. (I know, bees go for pollen, but honey sounded nicer).

What does it do for the reader? It guides them, it gives them a reference point, it makes the words less boring, it is more aesthetically pleasing, As I said before though, beware of too much colour, it can just as easily drive the reader away. Be aware of the impact of colours too. A lot of research into the impact of colours upon people's moods has been done.

RED. Physical

Positive: Physical courage, strength, warmth, energy, basic survival, 'fight or flight', stimulation, masculinity, excitement.

Negative: Defiance, aggression, visual impact, strain.

BLUE. Intellectual.

Positive: Intelligence, communication, trust, efficiency, serenity, duty, logic, coolness, reflection, calm.

Negative: Coldness, aloofness, lack of emotion, unfriendliness.

YELLOW. Emotional

Positive: Optimism, confidence, self-esteem, extraversion, emotional strength, friendliness, creativity.

Negative: Irrationality, fear, emotional fragility,

depression, anxiety, suicide.

GREEN. Balance

Positive: Harmony, balance, refreshment, universal love, rest, restoration, reassurance, environmental awareness, equilibrium, peace.

Negative: Boredom, stagnation, blandness.

VIOLET. Spiritual

Positive: Spiritual awareness, containment, vision, luxury, authenticity, truth, quality.

Negative: Introversion, decadence, suppression, inferiority.

ORANGE.

Positive: Physical comfort, food, warmth, security, sensuality, passion, abundance, fun.

Negative: Deprivation, frustration, frivolity, immaturity.

PINK.

Positive: Physical tranquillity, nurture, warmth, femininity, love, sexuality, survival of the species.

Negative: Inhibition, emotional claustrophobia, emasculation, physical weakness.

GREY.

Positive: Psychological neutrality.

Negative: Lack of confidence, dampness, depression, hibernation, lack of energy.

BLACK.

Positive: Sophistication, glamour, security, emotional safety, efficiency, substance.

Negative: Oppression, coldness, menace, heaviness.

WHITE.
Positive: Hygiene, sterility, clarity, purity, cleanness, simplicity, sophistication, efficiency.
Negative: Sterility, coldness, barriers, unfriendliness, elitism[12]

Now, bearing in mind that this is all true (further research on your part will confirm this) how confusing is it to see a word in an inappropriate colour? How about 'LOVE' in blue? 'COLD' in red? This can confuse the reader and the reader will not know why. Advertisers use tricks like this all the time. Just make sure that when you chose colours, you know why you have chosen them, what their purpose is.

L - Layout

In the same way that layout (or structure) is important for poems and prose, so it is for articles, the fronts of newspapers or leaflets.

Referring back to the article from the local paper, look how clean the layout is. Its silhouette is pleasing, so first impressions do not drive you away. It is laid out in clean, clearly defined columns, with regular text and a gradual change in text size and boldness. The text works well with the pictures and there is a flow to the article, which the eye is happy to follow.

You have to make it easy for the reader.

---

[12] www.colour-affects.co.uk

U - Underline

Why underline words? <u>To make them stand out.</u> That's it. I used this technique in the poems section where I wanted to highlight certain words.

My advice though, is don't overuse it. Too much and it looks tacky.

B - Bold text

Why have bold text? For the same reasons as underlining - **to make something stand out**. In the article, you will notice that the headline and sub-headline are in bold. The difference is in the font size. The editor wants both to stand out; he just wants one to stand out more than the other does.

B - Bullets

Word is great for bullets. It gives you a wide variety and allows you to add your own. You might have noticed my tiny feather icons in the book.

Bullets are for lists, to make things stand out, to index, to present order, to make things easier to understand. The article uses them to talk about the two different productions. It clarifies, simplifies.

Be consistent with them. Don't change them halfway through a list. If you use capitals on one, use capitals on all of them. Please the reader's eye.

PART SIX:
THE INTERNET

T'Interweb

Times they are a-changin', as Robert Zimmerman once said.

When I was younger, I can remember my father telling my sister and me that he'd had a nightmare and that, in that nightmare, he had been chased by the Zimmer Man. Weird. He was not, to my knowledge, a Bob Dylan fan.

If ever the phrase 'two-edged sword' was invented for anything, it was the internet. And swords, obvs.

The internet is a piece of genius. It allows people access to things that they would not have had access to prior to its invention. It spreads education, is perfect for what is known as 'rhizomatic learning', where communities spread knowledge, where everything is interconnected.

This opening up and broadening of knowledge is a wonderful thing. We now have access to more information than we have ever had and it is so easy. We are no longer restricted by political bias (depending on that country's censorship laws - China), to education being limited by your social status or income. We can link scientific knowledge over Skype or through instant messaging. We can see countries that we have never seen before through Google Maps or on CCTV cameras connected to the net. It is virtual travel.

And, you can bounce your book across the world in seconds.

The BBC had a wonderful program on a couple of years ago about India's frontier railways. A lad from Lahore in Pakistan had lost the sight in one eye due to an accident with some battery acid. His father was able to search on the net for someone who could treat him. They found someone in Delhi. For the first time in either of their lives, they travelled out of Pakistan, opening up their horizons with that trip alone, and the lad made a good recovery. It's a great story about the power of the internet and how it really can change lives.

As writers, we really should be making the most of the internet. It can do so much for us, from publishing to advertising and the thing is, there is really no excuse for not using it.

I am a Luddite. A lazy Luddite. Alliteratively so. It took me years to get a computer. It took me years to *appreciate* computers. It took me a ridiculous amount of time to set myself up a website (www.chrisbradburycreative.com, he preened).

The problem is that, if I didn't get to it, I was going to be left behind. Sometimes, it's better to jump on the bus, even if you don't know where it's going.

Younger people nowadays live on the net. TV watching no longer exists in the traditional way. They pick and choose what they want to see. Music is bought on MP3s, books are read on Kindle or a laptop. Technology is dictating the way we live in every possible way.

So, if you are serious about all this, get yourself a web page. You can pick them up for free today. Mine is through Wix, but there are others available.

On here, I have my prose, my poetry, my writing for kids, my photos, some music and art. It is free. Let me say that again - it is free. I can pay for more bells and whistles, but I don't need them. I can, via Wix, send out info sheets about new books to everyone in my contacts list. The biggest limitation is me. I have the design abilities of a monkey with a crayon. I need to work on it, but at least I'm out there.

I'm also on Facebook and Instagram.

I should make the effort to be on Twitter, but I don't like it. I once got lost on the internet because of

Twitter. It was cold and dark and frightening.

However, despite my own fears and incompetence, it is all but essential for any writer or artist to be on the internet; it takes some work and some patience but, come one, it is free publicity in a money-grabbing world. Take it while you can.

Blogging - and its cousin, vlogging - is another thing that we should be doing as writers.

Here are some interesting facts and figures:

72% of all internet users are now active on social media

18-29 year olds have an 89% usage

The 30-49 bracket sits at 72%

60 % of 50 to 60 year olds are active on social media

In the 65 plus bracket, 43% are using social media

71% of users access social media from a mobile device.

Social networks and blogging account for 12% of UK internet time

9% of US marketing companies employ a full-time blogger

55% of technology companies have acquired a customer through their company blogs

81% of US online consumers trust information and advice from blogs

181M+ blogs on the net

3 million new blogs every month

18 post updates every second

1.3M+ blogs every day

Over 60% of businesses have a blog

31% more bloggers today than in 2009
WordPress: 45% market share: 42,000,000 blogs: 500,000 new posts/day: 400,000 comments/day
Blogger: 35%
Tumblr: 9%
Others: 11%[13]

These figures might well have changed since I gathered them a short while ago, but it's a guarantee that they will have only increased. It's just not an area that we can afford to neglect.

Why Not Blog?

Some people do not like to put it out there. You don't have that excuse if you want to be a writer. So what reasons are there for not blogging?

- Lack of confidence - Who cares what you think? Your opinions aren't valid. You're not clever enough.
- Lack of technical expertise - Scared to go on the net? Not sure where to blog or what to blog?
- Lack of subject knowledge - You want to say something but think that you don't know enough.
- Lack of time – Work, kids, travel,

---

[13] jeffbullas.com and factbrowser.com and http://visual.ly/facts-and-figures-about-blogging

sleeping, eating, TV, reading, shopping, spouse, etc etc etc. If you can find time to write a book, you can find time to blog.

- Lack of web space - No there isn't!
- Lack of talent - Think you don't have the basic talent required to blog? Then why are you writing a book? Of course you have the talent. Don't confuse a lack of talent with a lack of application. That's you told.

Why Blog?

1. To Express Your Thoughts and Opinions:
You have something to say, and blogs provide a place to say it and be heard. I do tend to bang on about how important it is for people to have a voice. This will help you find it.

2. To Market or Promote Something:
Blogging is a great way to help market or promote yourself or your business, product or service.

3. To Help People:
Many blogs are written to help people who may be going through similar situations that the blogger has experienced. As a

writer, this is a great way to get through to potential readers.

4. To Establish Yourself as an Expert:
I don't think I'd have the balls to say I'm an expert at anything. Many people have though and I admire them for that. If you have the chutzpah, do it.

5. To Connect with People Like You:
I'm not a great mixer, but I accept wholeheartedly the idea that blogging brings like-minded people together. Starting a blog can help you find those people and share your opinions and thoughts and learn from them.

6. To Make a Difference:
I like(d) my job because I gained a sense of satisfaction. If I could go home knowing that I had made a difference, even in the smallest way, then I was happy. This idea can be expanded on the net via blogging. It can be political or practical or hobby-based. It can be what you want.

7. To Stay Active or Knowledgeable in a Field or Topic:
Since successful blogging is partially dependent on posting frequency and providing updated, fresh information, it's a perfect way to help a blogger stay abreast of the events in a specific field or topic.

8. To Stay Connected with Friends and Family:
There's also vlogging. Yes, that's a real thing. Video logging as opposed to web logging ('web logging' became abbreviated to 'blogging'). The world has become a small place. Use it.

9. To Make Money:
Yep. What else can you say? Just don't expect it.

10. To Have Fun and Be Creative:
Many people start a blog simply for fun. It is very good practice. Keeping up a blog requires regular writing and commitment. Anything that allows you to practice your art and gives you a bit of self-discipline can only help.

Writing is about finding freedom, not about finding constraints. It's about allowing yourself expression, giving yourself permission to mine for those diamonds inside. You can write a haiku or start a revolution...it is up to you.

PART SEVEN: PLOTTING
(Hang on a minute, lads. I've got a great idea...)[14]

---

[14] Name the film! If you don't know, feel shame.

If you are anything like me, you will spent days, weeks, with an idea spinning around in your head like a tornado, unrooted, uncatchable. As it spins, it begins to suck in other debris that flies through your mind until, heavy with ideas, too heavy to spin any more, it subsides and those ideas drop haphazardly to the ground.

All I have to do then is put them in some semblance of order.

Hence the little black notebook.

I hate planning. Once I have an idea, I like to just get on with it, but by doing that I often just end up down a dark country lane, freezing in the headlights like a mxyomatosed rabbit.

Here are a couple of ideas that I use to get the juices flowing.

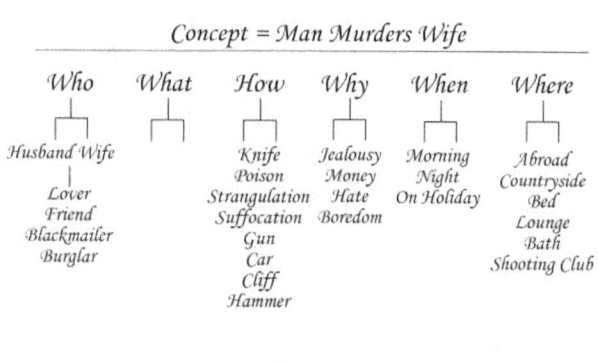

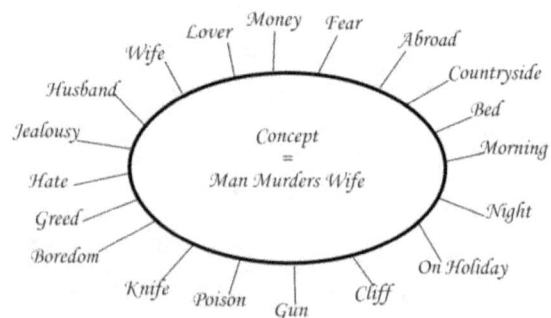

What they do is put those crazy disorganised thoughts into that order that they so crave.

In the first one, it asks the all-important 'who, what, how, why, when and where' questions. These, as any journalist will tell you, are the basics. Once you have your concept, break it down.

In the 'who' section, you can put the main protagonist or everyone, if you have thought that far ahead. You can add to the list as you go on.

The 'what' section, as you can see, is not needed at this stage. So why is it there? You could start off with a 'what on earth were they doing there?' at the beginning of the tale if you wish. As you delve deeper into your plot, many whats will occur and this is where you can keep a list of those unanswered questions.

'How' is self-explanatory. You are never going to run out of things to go here.

As for the 'why's, motives are also endless. The human creature is so fragile, so fickle, that almost any why will fit in here.

'When' gives you and the reader yet more choice. Was it in the blue of midnight, in the hot, high sun of the desert at midday or on holiday, away from the prying eyes of the neighbours, when accidents just sometimes happen?

'Where' is up to you. I set *The High Commissioner's Wife* on an island in the middle of the Indian Ocean because I happened to live on one many years ago. The world is your oyster. Just remember to do your research. Thoroughly.

The spider diagram below says the same thing, just set out in a different way. It depends how you like to work, but some sort of rigid foundation to build your book upon is an essential, whether it be fiction or non-fiction.

It is not possible to give you a peachy answer to

this. We are all different; we all have different likes and dislikes.

The important thing to remember is that, with proper planning, you can always get something together. Anyone can write.

My notebook, full of crossings out and ideas. A great companion on my journey. These were two of many pages for *The High Commissioner's Wife*, jotted down hurriedly between biscuits, no doubt. Please note the drawing of the church. I drifted.

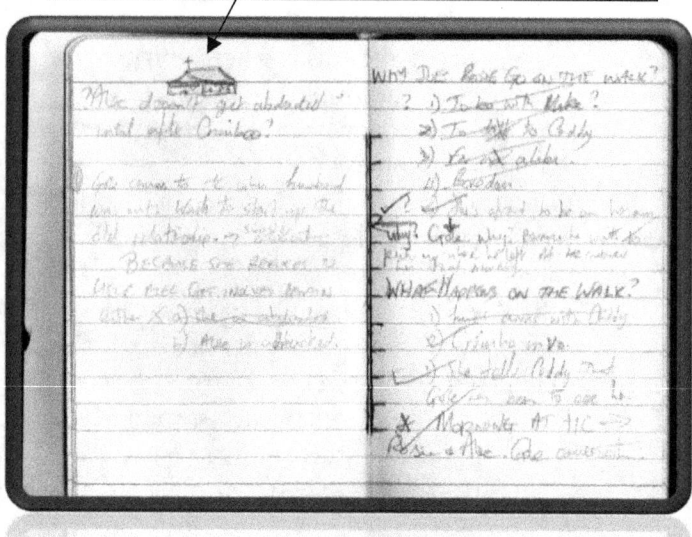

PART EIGHT:
OTHER STUFF

Punctuation

This is when the class falls asleep. You can see it happening. Heads drop. Hands come up to support heads. Hands collapse. Heads fall forward into desk. Hands and arms are neatly folded to create a warm, comfortable pillow.

I sat next to a student who actually started to snore. He was leaning back in the chair in that snapped neck position, fly-catching. If he hadn't snored, he would still be there now, a bleached skeleton. Asleep.

So what is the point of punctuation? All it does it get students in a tizzy and give English teachers a stroke. Do we really need it?

Yes, we do really. Much like the DAFOREST and THE MOIST PEARS techniques, punctuation will allow your reader to understand you. What is the point of spending hours, days and months writing something, only for the world not to understand what the hell you're jabbering on about? There is no point.

Think of enjambment. It is such a vital part of poetry, not just in the interpretation, but in the reading and therefore the comprehension, that we couldn't do without it. Absence of punctuation is essentially punctuation. It's that old thing about the silences between the notes.

✎ **Full stops** divide sentences from other sentences.

'He ate a banana. He vomited a short time later.'

(Just putting in my own dislike of fruit. It's all about experience this writing lark, you know)

✎ **Question marks** are used in the place of full stops

when the sentence is a question.

'Did you vomit after eating that banana?'

In speech, the question mark goes inside the quotation marks and you can end the sentence there. Do not use a full stop and a question mark. It is not necessary. It is sinful.

Exclamation marks are used after words, phrases or sentences that are exclamatory.

'I can't believe that you vomited that lovely banana!'

Never do this:

'I CAN'T BELIEVE THAT YOU VOMITED THAT LOVELY BANANA!?!'

It is against the law and you can be prosecuted under the Decency Act. This might not be true, but don't do it anyway. It is amateurish.

Colons are used for lists or to separate parts of a sentence where that which comes after the colon is a summary of what came before.

'He wiped the mess from around his mouth: he had eaten and vomited my banana.'

Semicolons In their book, *My Grammar and I*, Caroline Taggart and JA Wines describe semicolons as Supercommas. I like that. A lot.

They describe semicolon as being something that 'connects two independent clauses that don't quite justify being a sentence in their own right. It often replaces *and* or *but*.'

I often say that if you don't know whether to put a comma or full stop, use a semicolon.

'You have eaten my banana; I bet you're sick.'

It could have been:

'You have eaten my banana and I bet you're sick.'

Or

'You have eaten my banana. I bet you're sick.'

To be honest, I think they're all great. Supercommas can mess with your head. Don't let them. Go with your instinct. If you're wrong, you'll soon find out.

Dashes are used to indicate a pause or to introduce a list or explanation. I often use them.

'That banana - my banana - is gone. Where is it?'

Hyphens are used in some compound words such as 'musk-rose' and 'non-infectious'. If you want to join what are usually two separate words together, use a hyphen.

'You are a yellow banana thief.'

'You are a yellow-banana thief.'

In the first sentence, the thief is yellow. In the second example, the banana is yellow. He will not steal green bananas and will probably to his best to avoid overripe ones too.

Another good example is 'deep blue sea.' In other words, the sea is deep *and* blue. However, deep-blue sea means that the colour of the sea is deep blue.

Hyphens can change meanings, so be careful.

- **Parentheses** (brackets to you and me). 'Parentheses (always used in pairs) allow a writer to provide additional information. The parenthetical material might be a single word, a fragment, or multiple complete sentences. Whatever the material inside the parentheses, it must not be grammatically integral to the surrounding sentence. This is an easy mistake to avoid. Simply read your sentence without the parenthetical content. If it makes sense, the parentheses are acceptable; if it doesn't, the punctuation must be altered.'[15]

'My banana (and it was *my* banana) is gone.'

- **Commas** are there to help the reader breathe. It can present a space for a pause or separate two different parts of a sentence.

---

[15] www.thepunctuationguide.com

'The banana, which is my favourite fruit, has been eaten.'

'You must understand, that banana was mine.'

'The panda eats shoots and leaves.'
'The panda eats, shoots and leaves.' [16]

> Comma alert!

The whole context is changed. We go from cuddly ursine pal to 'gangsta panda' with a single comma. That may be fine for Quentin Tarantino, but not for a bunch of five year olds in Mrs Kemp's class. Be clear about what is happening to whom and when.

Quotation marks are used for speech. Many people use these. " ". I use these, ' '.

'You stole my banana,' she said. 'You owe me one banana.'

Apostrophes. 'Whose banana is it? It's Peter's banana.'

OMG! This is where students actually slip into a coma. It messes with their heads so badly that it scrambles their brain and they have to have beer to revive them.
Let's take it a bit at a time.

---

[16] *Eats, Shoots and Leaves* by Lynne Truss – Fourth Estate. Possibly the grammar bible.

'It's' = 'it is'
'There's' = 'there is'

The writer puts the apostrophe where the abbreviation is.

That's easy, yes?

Now we come to the possessive apostrophe.

'Peter's Banana' = the banana belonging to Peter.

'Grandma's teeth are missing' = the teeth that are missing belong to grandma.

It's (it is) about who owns what.

What about words that end in 's'? I hear you scream.

James' banana

or

James's banana

Either will do.

In the plural, stick the apostrophe on the end.

'It is the boys' bunch of bananas.' = The bunch of bananas belongs to more than one boy.

'The girls' dresses.' = The dresses belong to more

than one girl.

If the word is already plural, eg children or people, all you do is this:

Children's
People's

(I love this. Word has just told me off for using the possessive)

Here is a sentence with them all:

'I'm sure it's James's banana, but it might be the children's.'

Have a look and differentiate the uses of the apostrophes. You'll find it's not too difficult.

One more thing –

'It's' and 'its'.
The possessive form of 'its' no longer has an apostrophe in it. Only put one in if you abbreviate 'it is'.

I don't make the rules. It's not my fault.

Paragraphs

I want to say something here about paragraphs. I know that they don't strictly come under punctuation, but they are so abused and misused that I feel the need to leap randomly to their defence.

What is a paragraph?

A paragraph is a unit of text that represents a new stage in the written piece.

A new paragraph is created when there is a significant pause in the writing, which signifies to the reader a new subject or a new slant upon the theme. Each paragraph should contain its own content, its own ideas, but remain within the central theme of the chapter.

A change of subject altogether usually calls for a new chapter.

What it does is it let the reader know that there is a slight change of direction coming up, but that it will not stray from the main theme of that chapter. It might introduce a twist of events within that chapter, but you wouldn't, for example, if writing a book about pets, suddenly lurch from Chihuahuas to Lionfish within the space of a paragraph.

It also breaks up the page and stops the reader being overfaced by a relentless block of text.

Here's an example: from *The Stilling of the Heart*

'Beyond that line lay everything. Beyond that line lay dragons and dreams. He imagined himself upon the prow of a ship as it sliced the waves and headed resolutely towards mystery. Across that thin horizon lay promise and adventure and the start of something new.

Behind him lay the past and he knew that he would not go back. It had created him as surely as his mother's wo

Around him flew the guns. They cheered

Change of subject within the main theme

him, urged him onwards to the places that even they dared not go.

| New theme, new chapter | Chapter Thirteen |

The surgery was a converted turn of the century house. It was an impressive building. Stairs swept from the glass and chrome reception area.'

Homonyms and Homophones

Homonyms are words that are spelled the same, but have different meanings.

Here are some examples:

Entrance – 1. to captivate 2. A way in
Pole – 1. Someone from Poland 2. A big stick-type thing.
Beam – 1. To smile broadly 2. A piece of wood that stops your house falling around your neck.
Toast – 1. Cooked bread 2. To raise a glass to

Beware of words with more than one meaning. They can trip you up. Word processors will sometimes notice them, but often they will offer you the incorrect alternative.

Homophones are words that sound the same, but are spelt differently and have different meaning.

Here are some examples:

They're Their There

Pear Pare
Bear Bare
Floured Flowered

These are common and avoidable errors and, if made, can be fatal to the integrity of the written piece/peace. Watch out.

Easily confused words

This is such an enormous list. Bill Bryson or the Great Bill, as he is known in this household, wrote a book about them called *Troublesome Words*. That's how many there are. They needed a whole book to themselves. The great thing is, you actually see Bill going red as he writes in infuriated fashion about each one. I would recommend getting a copy. It's a great education, as are most of his works.

Here are some of the more common ones.

Accept to agree to receive or do
Except not including

Affect to change or make a difference to; with reference to an emotional state, hence 'affective disorder' and 'affection'.
Effect a result; to bring about a result;

Aloud out loud
Allowed permitted

Currant a dried grape
Current happening now; a flow of water, air, or electricity

Discreet careful not to attract attention
Discrete separate and distinct

Foreword an introduction to a book
Forward onwards, ahead

Principal The head of the school or college
Principle A fundamental belief

Stationery Pens, papers, staples etc
Stationary Standing still

This is but a few of the common errors dotted across the pages of thousands of writers. Including me.

The Parts of Speech and Writing.

A sentence must have certain elements within it to be classed as a sentence. These are

1)   Subject 2) Verb 3) Object

'The cat sat on the mat.'

Now, which parts of it are which?

The verb, clearly, is 'sat'.
The object is whatever is at the receiving end of

the verb. In this case, it's the mat.

The subject is the person/living being doing the verb. That would be the cat.

Here's another sentence.

'The car died on the motorway.'

    1) Subject 2) Verb 3) Object

'The car died on the motorway.'

This is why we need the parts of speech - to help us construct sentences which everyone can understand. We take them for granted, but when you read a piece of work by someone who hasn't yet grasped the concept, you will see what I mean.

Finally, a sentence should deal with one topic. If you change subject hallway through a sentence, the banana was delicious.

See what I mean?

So, what are the parts of speech?

Adjectives
Nouns
Verbs
Pronouns
Adverbs
Prepositions
Conjunctions
Imperatives

Adjectives

An adjective is a word that that describes a noun (or pronoun).

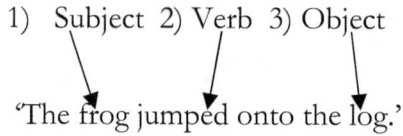

'The frog jumped onto the log.'

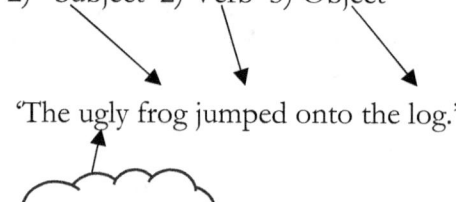

'The ugly frog jumped onto the log.'

That's it. Really. How complicated do you want it to be?

Nouns

A noun is a name. It can be a proper noun or a common noun

A proper noun starts with a capital letter; a common noun does not.

Common nouns can be broken down into Abstract and Concrete nouns.

Abstract nouns deal with those things beyond the senses such as courage, desire, democracy, happiness, curiosity, peace, love, fear and other emotions.

Concrete nouns are nouns that deal with the five senses, unless you're Spiderman, then Bob's your uncle. If the noun does not deal with the senses, it is not a concrete noun.

Proper nouns are such as: Brian, Peter, Jenny, Salisbury, Hertfordshire, God, Persil.

Common nouns are such as: school, church, dog, bicycle, dinner.

Nouns can be broken down further into sub-groups. That's good, isn't it.

Honestly, just worry about whether they have a capital letter at the front of them or not (and any apostrophes).

Capital letter = Proper noun
No capital letter = Common noun.

Verbs

Verbs are 'doing' words e.g. eating, drinking, sleeping.

I sleep,
You sleep,
He/she/it sleeps, — Singular

We sleep,
You sleep,
They sleep. — Plural

Just remember your verb in relation to your subject and your object and you're there.

The other thing to watch out for, and it's an easy mistake to make, is tense. Don't drift from present to past to future tense and confuse the reader. It sounded daft, but it will be an easy thing to do.

Pronouns

These are words that replace nouns – he, she it, they etc.

They can be separated, if you really, really want, into subject pronouns and object pronouns.

Subject Pronouns
I, she, he, you, it, we, they

Object Pronouns
Me, you, him, her, it, us, them

Don't worry too much about the types for now but from writer's perspective they are very handy because they avoid the constant need to repeat names and therefore add a bit of colour to your writing.

'Janet went to the shops. Janet bought some chocolate. Janet then went home.'

'Janet went to the shops. She bought some chocolate. She went home.'

The second version is more interesting.
The example I chose to use was really, *really* dull.

Adverbs

An adverb describes a verb, adjective or adverb
There is a general rule that can be applied here - adverbs end in '-ly'.

He peeled the banana <u>quickly</u>.
He ate the banana <u>slowly</u>.
He vomited <u>rapidly</u>.

There is however a slight caveat. Not all words that end in '-ly' are adverbs. Butterfly is not an adverb. The other warning is that not all adverbs end in '-ly'.

Over the page is a useful 'Adverb Mat'[17], which shows adverb usage. It's a clever list but it's not the kind of thing that you should worry about when starting out.

---

[17] www.twinkl.co.uk

Adverbs

How?

angrily
anxiously
cautiously
cheerfully
courageously
crossly
cruelly
defiantly
doubtfully
elegantly
enthusiastically
foolishly
frantically
gently
gladly
gracefully
happily
hungrily
inquisitively
irritably
joyously
loudly
madly
merrily
nervously
quickly
sadly
safely
shyly
solemnly
weakly
well
wildly

When?

afterwards
again
before
beforehand
early
lately
never
now
often
punctually
recently
soon
then
today
tomorrow
yesterday

How often?

always
annually
constantly
daily
hourly
monthly
never
occasionally
often
once
regularly
repeatedly
sometimes
usually
yearly

Where?

above
around
away
below
down
downstairs
everywhere
here
inside
outside
there
up
upstairs
wherever

How much?

almost
completely
entirely
little
much
rather
totally
very

More useful adverbs...

additionally	appropriately	consequently
fittingly	hence	however
insufficiently	suitably	therefore

twinkl www.twinkl.co.uk

Prepositions

Going back to our simplistic sentence:

'The cat sat on the mat.'

The preposition is 'on'.
A preposition is there to tell the reader the place of the subject.

'The frog jumped onto the log.'

'Onto' is the preposition.

So, think of place and subject and you have your preposition. Other prepositions include:[18]

Of In To For With On At From By About As Into Like Through After Over Between Out Against During Without Before Under Around Among

Conjunctions

Conjunctions are joining words.

'The cat. The dog. The sparrow.'
'The cat <u>and</u> the dog <u>and</u> the sparrow.'

The boy survived. The banana didn't.
The boy survived <u>but</u> the banana didn't

There are four types of conjunctions. I immediately regret saying that because I'm going to have to tell you

---

[18] www.englishclub.com the 25 most common prepositions.

what they are and possibly overface you.

They are: co-ordinating, sub-ordinating, correlative and compound. Do not worry about that yet.

Here are some commonly conjunctions used that come from all groups and are in no particular order.

> And Or But Nor So For Yet After Although As If As Long As Because Before Even If Even Though If Once Provided Since So That Till Unless Until What When Whenever Wherever Whether While

What good are conjunctions to a writer? Quite simply, they make your sentences more interesting, they add colour, variety and stimulate the reader. They stop you as the writer getting bored. Often, they are a good way to start a new sentence or paragraph. It's all about keeping the attention of the reader.

Imperatives

Stop! Get off! Eat! Run!

These are imperatives, also known as interjections. They are usually followed by an exclamation mark.

That is all I have to say about that.[19]

---

[19] Run, Forrest! Run!

PART NINE
PUBLISHING

Publishing

Hands up who hasn't heard of Catch 22?

It's a famous book by Joseph Heller. In it, the protagonist wants to get out of the war in which he is submerged.

He therefore claims that he is mad so that he can be discharged from military service.

The military says that if you know you are mad, you cannot be mad.

Catch 22.

How does this apply to writing?

You want a publisher. You cannot get a publisher without having an agent. You won't get an agent unless you've been published.

Catch 22.

On top of this, since the recession of 2008 and the big changes that have come about since the introduction of e-readers, changing the paperback/hardback market drastically, especially profit-wise, publishers have been reluctant to invest in anything but a sure thing. That is why you see so many celebrity books - the public will buy anything if it's by a celebrity.

By all means though, hoick your work around to agents and publishers, but be prepared for rejection. I have had more rejections than Quasimodo at the Playboy dinner. It's hard and heart-breaking.

With the advent of the internet comes something old with a new twist upon it. The self-publisher.

A few years ago, quite rightly, this was a dirty, grubby little phrase and there are still unscrupulous publishers out there willing to charge you to publish your work. If they ask you for money, tell them to piss off. Seriously. No self-respecting publisher does this. This is why it was/is called 'vanity publishing' - people did it because they just wanted to say that they had published a book or were desperate to do so because they had invested so much time and effort into their work.

Now things have changed.

Apart from the desperation. That thrives like a demon.

What do these writers and their books have in common?

10. David Chilton – The Wealthy Barber

9. James Redfield – The Celestine Prophecy

8. K.A Tucker – Ten Tiny Breaths

7. Michael J. Sullivan – The Riyria Chronicles

6. H.M Ward – Damaged

5. Barbara Freethy – Daniel's Gift

4. Lisa Genova – Still Alice

3. Amanda Hocking

2. Hugh Howey – Wool Trilogy

1. E.L James – 50 Shades of Grey[20]

Yep. They were all self-published. They are all serious writers who, for whatever reason, could not get their books out the traditional way, so did it themselves.

I think that's fabulous.

I publish through Amazon and because that is the one I know, I'll show you how.

There are of course other e-publishers available. I would advise you to take a look at them because the more you know, the greater your choice.[21]

When I first started with Amazon, there were two

---

[20] www.therichest.com

[21] eg Kobo, Lulu. www.publishersweekly.com has an extensive list of those available.

distinct categories: Createspace for paperbacks and Kindle for eBooks. Amazon have now, quite sensibly, put them both under the Amazon/KDP umbrella so that there is a link between the eBook and the paperback. You just have to go to one place to find both.

Go to the Amazon webpage. At the bottom of the page you will see a section called 'Make Money with Us' and within that, 'Independently Publish with Us'. Click on that and follow the instructions.

Open an account and away you go.

The rest is child's play, really and it will cost you not one bean.

I have used two sizes of book - 6" x 9" and 5.25" x 8". I stopped using the 6x9 simply because I didn't like the look of it. I now do 5.25 x 8 all the time.

What you must do is get the margins right. I'll show you what measurements I use for my 5.25 x 8 books (see below).

It can be fiddly, it can be annoying, but it can also be very satisfying. Also, Amazon give you a lot of help by providing templates for books. They are a business and that is their job, but they do it well and all communications up to this point have been excellent and prompt.

I design my own covers too. Once again, Amazon are very helpful and provide templates and flexibility. When you hand in your project, they will not let you get away with substandard material. If you have done it wrong, they will tell you and expect you to do it right. They will do their best to help you put out a good piece of work.

They will also guide you towards getting your book onto Kindle.

The Kindle is a separate concept from the paperback. It is there to enable e-publishing and therefore has ideas of its own, such as promotion and advertising.

What about royalties?

I am paid monthly by Kindle. Below you can see how the royalties work in Kindle. They have been criticised for a lack of generosity, but if you latch onto something like '*50 Shades of Grey*,' it soon mounts up. I choose to put my Kindle books on at this price in order to sell them. It works for some and not for others. Just try it.

Don't be greedy. Use your common sense and be prepared to compromise.

Writing is a hobby that, if you are lucky, might turn into a job.

Please select a royalty option for your book. (What's this?)

- ◉ 35% Royalty
- ○ 70% Royalty

	List Price	Royalty Rate	Delivery Costs	Estimated Royalty
Amazon.com	$ 0.99 USD Price must be between $0.99 and $200.00.	35%	n/a	$0.35
Amazon.co.uk	☐ Set UK price automatically based on US price £ 0.99 GBP Price must be between £0.99 and £150.00. (£0.83 without UK VAT)	35%	n/a	£0.29*
Amazon.de	☑ Set DE price automatically based on US price €0.99 (€0.83 without DE VAT)	35%	n/a	€0.29*
Amazon.fr	☑ Set FR price automatically based on US price €0.99 (€0.84 without FR VAT)	35%	n/a	€0.33*
Amazon.es	☑ Set ES price automatically based on US price €0.99 (€0.82 without ES VAT)	35%	n/a	€0.29*

Finally, I want to take you into the future.

Writers can do that you know.

This is the e-mail I received from Amazon telling me about the work that I had submitted for this book:

'To
xxxxxx@xxxxxx

The interior and cover files for A Beginner's Guide to ..., #xxxxxxx have been reviewed.

The cover file does not meet our submission requirements for the reason(s) listed below. Please make any necessary adjustments to your cover file and upload it again.

We are unable to place a barcode on your cover due to live elements/graphics appearing within in the lower right-hand corner of your back cover. Please adjust the back cover so that no images or text intended to be viewable are placed in this location. Allow a space 2.0" wide and 1.2" tall for the barcode placement.

The spine text is too large for the page count and may wrap to the front or back cover. Please reduce the font size and center the spine text, ensuring that there is at least 0.0625" of room on either side.

The Interior file meets our submission requirements; it is not necessary for you to make any revisions to this file or upload it again.

Our reviewers did find some non-blocking issues with your files. Some of these issues may have been fixed causing alterations to your files.

The interior contains transparency which is flattened during our processing and may result in a slight change in appearance.

The interior contains images that are less than 200 DPI; these may appear blurry or pixelated when printed. For more information on image resolution, visit our Help page.

Best regards'

See what I mean? Polite and to the point, all the time offering help and alternatives. I will now have to hop into the future and make these changes.

Whichever service you choose to publish on or if you are lucky enough to find a publisher willing to commit, good luck.

This is how your KDP page will look once you have gone and done the dirty deed. It is quite satisfying to see your hard work given legs at last.

You will note that, from here, you have input to both the Kindle version of your book and your paperback. From here you can do all the editing you want.

Amazon has various tools to promote your book, some free, some not. It is always a good idea to have a free giveaway of your book when it is first released. Once again, it is free publicity and could potentially lead to sales through word of mouth.

What's it all about, Alfie?

Finishing your book is, of course, only the beginning. You must sell it and this is probably the most difficult task of all. There is plenty of advice out there as to how you should go about this, but it is hard work, especially if you are also holding down a full time job.

It's about presenting a whole, cohesive, honest piece of work, be it prose, poetry, an article for a magazine or a piece for your night class.

It is about presentation and that only works with good planning and preparation. You cannot have a man standing up only to find out two sentences later that he's not yet out of bed. You cannot set a book in WWII and have Concorde passing over. These things matter. So ask yourself what and who the story is about. Refer to those plans that I nagged you about. Ask yourself what this person's problem is. Where are they? And why? Are you telling their story in the first person or the third person? Consistency matters. If necessary, do the research. If you fail, you will shatter the illusion.

It's also about structure. A piece of work not only has to be intellectually pleasing, but it has to be aesthetically pleasing. There is nothing worse than wading through some homogenous claptrap when trying to follow a plot or a conversation or trying to remain attentive when presented with a block of uninspiring text.

The writer must present the perfect off the peg, fit-to-a-tee, suit of words that the reader can find.

Plan. Write. Revise. Refine.

It's about grammar. Then some grammar. Then

some more grammar.

'He slowly took her stockings off.'

Say what? Why was he wearing her stockings? Oh, I see.

It's not about being picky or splitting hairs, it's about being crystal clear.

Do your research, double-check your facts and make sure that you know your English. Unless you're writing in French. Then don't worry.

When you get up in the morning you might, like me, look in the mirror and feel a certain sense of regret.

There is also a slight concern that I have to make that wrinkly, bush-haired, bag-eyed wreck presentable.

So I wash, clean my teeth, brush my hair, get dressed in clothes that, by middle-aged male standards, are deemed acceptable in the outside world.

Then, during the day, I collect all the things that make me who and what I am - the TV news, the newspaper, getting the kids up, the journey to work, the interaction with colleagues and friends, a good or bad lunch, meetings, letters, e-mails, arguments, smiles, tears, the journey home...

At the end of the day, I am a different person to the one who started it. For good or bad, I've added colour to my life and those colours are different to the ones with which I woke up.

I am defined.

Such is your book. Allow it to roll in the rainbow. If your ideas change, let it happen. The boundaries are *your* boundaries. Walk up to them, give them a push and, if they bend a little, extend them.

Remember though, too little colour is dull. Too

much colour is blinding.

These things might all seem very small, but small things can carry a lot of weight.

When it comes to writing, if you can get all these elements together - the characters, the place, the pace, the time, the grammar, the words, the plot, the concept - then your work will carry weight.

Most of all, it's about finding your boundaries and smashing through them. It's about finding your limitations and then rendering them non-existent. It's about freedom to think and say what you like and at the same time to broaden your mind.

Writing changes things. Let it change you.

And finally:

Just write...

ABOUT THE AUTHOR

Chris Bradbury was born in 1962. He attended schools in Bracknell, Windsor, Mauritius and Bloxham and, despite all these, failed to learn a thing. He spent his formative years in a cocoon and failed to see the time go by. When he woke up, he realised that it was too late.

He has been a shop worker, a hospital porter, worked in medical records, in the CSSD department, as an estate agent, as a nurse, as a delivery driver, a bus driver and as a teaching assistant.

He lives in Yorkshire.

He is married to a lady and has some lady children.

He loves them.

He is also the author of:

The High Commissioner's Wife
The Devil Inside
Catfish
No Time to Repent
Semper Occultus
Mayflies
Eidolon
The Stilling of the Heart
Shorts - A collection of novellas
Condition of Life - The Poetic Confessions of a Grumpy Old Man
The Ghost of Dormy Place and Other Tales
The Ashes of an Oak
A Kind and Gentle Man
Praxis (Sci-Fi Fantasy - with Ian Makinson)
Praxis - Part Two: Regeneration Paradox (Sci-Fi Fantasy -

with Ian Makinson)
Praxis - Part Three: The Liar's truth - (Sci-Fi Fantasy - with Ian Makinson)
Earthbound
Earthbound Part Two - Hellbound
Chine (Horror)
Uncomfortably Numb (Play)
The Scarlet Darter (fiction for children)
Unton's Teeth and Other Tales of Wordful Mystification (poems for children)
Phoenix - A Look at the Causes of World War Two
A Beginner's Guide to the Wars of the Roses
A Beginner's Guide to Creative Writing
A Beginner's Guide to Death